My Freshman Year

What a Professor Learned by Becoming a Student

Rebekah Nathan

CORNELL UNIVERSITY PRESS

Ithaca & London

First published 2005 by Cornell University Press

Printed in the United States of America

Library of Congress Cataloging-in-Publication Data

Nathan, Rebekah.
    My freshman year : what a professor learned by becoming a student / by Rebekah Nathan.
        p. cm.
    Includes bibliographical references and index.
    ISBN 0–8014–4397–0 (cloth : alk. paper)
  1. College students—United States—Social conditions—21st century.
2. Adult college students—United States—Social conditions—21st century.
I. Title.
    LB3605.N34   2005
    378.1'98—dc22   2005002213

Cornell University Press strives to use environmentally responsible suppliers and materials to the fullest extent possible in the publishing of its books. Such materials include vegetable-based, low-VOC inks and acid-free papers that are recycled, totally chlorine-free, or partly composed of nonwood fibers. For further information, visit our website at www.cornellpress.cornell.edu.

Cloth printing   10 9 8 7 6 5 4 3 2

Contents

Preface

The idea for doing this research really gelled after I audited a couple of courses for my own continuing interest and education. In two different semesters I sat in on a course offered in other departments, so naturally I went to class regularly, did course readings, and occasionally raised my hand to ask questions like everyone else in class. I discovered that in doing so I inherited a sort of transactional student identity. That is, because I related to the teacher as if I were a student, and behaved as students do, my default identity became that of a student. I found out quite unwittingly that if I walked like a duck and quacked like a duck . . . then people thought I was a duck. My fellow students began sharing opinions and gossip with me that I would never hear as a professor.

That was the beginning of my realization that, even after my fiftieth birthday, I could still be a student, and be treated by other students as, more or less, a peer. This new identity seemed essential to my budding research idea. While others had successfully studied campus life as professors, I wanted to see the campus through student eyes to the extent that was possible. I certainly did *not* want to relate to my classmates or residence hall mates or professors under a professorial identity. It was dramatically apparent to me that I heard a *very* different set of conversations when I audited classes than when I taught them, and I didn't want my research to digress into the often scripted dialogues that characterize professor-student discourse. I felt that the world I wanted to penetrate would be precluded if I were simply an interested professor "doing research" on students. I decided then to *become* a student by formally applying to the university, by registering for and taking courses, and by moving into a dorm—hence setting the stage to view undergraduate life as both an observer-interviewer and a participant.

A book about a professor who goes back to school as a freshman at her own university—not telling anyone that she's a professor—raises many questions, especially for ethnographers and students of ethnography. Can an anthropologist legitimately go "undercover"? Did the researcher lie to people about who she was? Did the university give her permission to do this? How did she deal with the requirements of her Institutional Research Board? Did anyone discover her real identity? And then there are methodological and presentational questions. Can a researcher who has not fully disclosed her identity record *any* of her own personal experiences in her field notes? Anything that anyone has said in her presence? Can she publish these accounts? As one reviewer of the manuscript suggested, ethnography should rely primarily on what natives say and how they say it. Why, then, are some chapters of this ethnography replete with quotations while others are thick with the author's own narrative? To add to the quandary is the question of anonymity. After much deliberation, I chose in the end to identify neither my university nor my own name. How is the reader to make sense of these choices?

Although I address some of these questions in the text, I want to give fuller play to these issues for those who wish to know more. I have done so in an appended afterword, titled "Ethics and Ethnography," where I discuss, among other things, my decision to write this book about "AnyU," an invented acronym, under a pseudonym, "Rebekah Nathan."

Such a decision complicates things, everything from the author's ability to respond to academic critique to her personal acknowledgments. To keep my identity unknown, I can send my thank-you's only to first names: to Linda, Kay, and Claudia for their early feedback and encouragement on the manuscript; to Dick for his brave and trusting facilitation of my classroom research; to Ann, from public radio, who helped me chronicle and reflect on my own experiences; to Phyllis for her year-long support and patience through my dorm experience; to my niece Rebekah and my nephew Nathan, both future college students, who lent me their names; and for the wonderful students at AnyU, who tutored, advised, helped, and inspired me as a student.

There is one person I can thank with a full name. I owe a special debt of gratitude to Frances Benson, editor at Cornell University Press. Our relationship is the sort one envisions authors and editors to have but they rarely do—a cooperative, generative, honest, and ongoing relationship that feeds the creative process. When the research behind this book was just a vague idea in my mind, Fran sat with me in Washington, D.C., for hours, listening, finally urging me to take the risk of breaking with my lifelong research agenda and moving forward with this ethnography. When this book was just an outline, Fran met me in New York City to discuss its development. When it was a completed manuscript, she slogged with me through issues of anonymity, which can be so troublesome to an academic press. May every professor who writes a book find such an editor and intellectual partner.

My Freshman Year

CHAPTER 1

Welcome to "AnyU"

Ten years ago, I would never have expected to be writing a book about college life at AnyU. I am a cultural anthropologist, and have spent most of my professional life living overseas in a remote village location (unnamed to preserve *all* our anonymity), learning the language and customs of another culture. As a traditional cultural anthropologist, I participated in and observed village life over a period of many years, joining village organizations, interviewing locals, and establishing long-term personal relationships. I wrote "ethnography," or descriptive accounts of the day-to-day life of a people, hoping to capture the intimate dynamics of social life and culture change. It is quite a leap from life in a village to life in the dorms, but perhaps I can offer a little explanation of how this book came about.

Anyone who has spent much time overseas knows that this experience makes you reconsider your own culture. You become an observer of what was once just lived. On your return from another world, things once unnoticed—our reliance on date books, for instance—seem glaring; what was a daily routine can resurface as an exotic American custom. Since my time overseas, I find myself constantly taking apart the taken-for-granted world in which I live, a penchant I eventually developed into a course on American culture. In it, I direct my students to look at their own culture with an anthropologist's eye, to reexamine its issues and its perplexities with the same sense of freshness and compassion and relativity they would bring to another culture. I decided to take my own advice as I thought about my academic experience.

After more than fifteen years of university teaching, I found that students had become increasingly confusing to me. Why don't undergraduates ever drop by for my office hours unless they are in dire trouble in a course? Why don't they respond to my (generous) invitations to do out-of-class research under my guidance? How could some of my students never take a note during my big lecture class? And what about those students who bring whole meals and eat and drink during class? Or those other students who seem to feel absolutely no embarrassment in putting their head or their feet on their desk and taking a nap during class?

I found myself laughing along with Carolyn Segal's tongue-in-cheek article about student excuses for late work and missed classes, including the ubiquitous "my roommate was throwing up blood."[1] I saw considerable truth in another published lament by a Duke University professor, who questioned the quality of undergraduate education even at his elite institution.[2]

I began to notice my own and colleagues' discourse as we continually tried to make sense of what seemed bizarre behavior. Were we like that? Are students today different? Doesn't it seem like they're . . . cheating more? ruder? less motivated? more steeped in their own sense of entitlement? Why is the experience of leading class discussions sometimes like pulling teeth? Why won't my students read the assigned readings so we can have a decent class discussion? The list goes on, despite the fact that we had other stories, too, of students hungry to learn, of "aha!" experiences, and of letters of thanks that arrived two years after a course ended.

Students' attitudes about their education had special significance to me in light of the student-centered mantras of contemporary universities. Professors across the country increasingly hear university administrators who speak like corporate managers, who believe that they are competing in an educational marketplace for student-consumers. Beyond making housing, registration, and like matters more student-friendly, university administrators are changing the nature of course delivery, pedagogy, scheduling, and degree offerings to address students' tastes and desires and thereby draw more applicants. In this climate, what students want and how they understand their education are becoming more central to the shape of the modern university.

A final impetus for this research came when I sat in on a couple of colleagues' courses that I had long wanted to audit informally. With the permission of the instructors, I attended a computer programming class and a class in Buddhism, courses obviously quite different in their content and in the students attracted to them. I came to class regularly, took notes, and did the readings, although I skipped the papers, tests, and other evaluative measures. In retrospect, I suppose that behaviors such as writing in a spiral notebook, raising my hand to ask a question, and sitting in class waiting for the instructor to arrive marked me as a student, even if I was an old one. To my surprise, I began to hear a new discourse as I was engaged by other students in conversation:

"Psst . . . psst . . . , excuse me . . . were you in class on Friday? Listen, I cut out and went skiing. Can I borrow your notes?"

"Hey, do you know what he said was going to be on the test? I was zoned out while he was telling us."

"Do you think it's fair that we have both the essay and the test in one week?"

It dawned on me soon enough that I had gone through the looking glass, so to speak, and I was now privy to a world that my students typically didn't share with me. I heard about weekend parties, and how someone wrote the paper drunk between 3 and 4:30 in the morning, and how unfair the grading was, and why did we have to take so many liberal studies courses anyway? The discourse I began to hear happened naturally in my shared status as student, and the difference in the content, formality, and tone of the dialogues struck me. I found myself writing down little snippets in my course notebook to remind myself after class of the conversation topics. "I mean, when are you ever gonna use Nietzsche at a cocktail party?" was one of my first notations from someone who obviously didn't feel that a philosophy course was worth the time.

I realized that I was starting to do ethnography, and to look at my experience with an anthropologist's eye; it was then that the idea of actually becoming a student occurred to me as a research project for my sabbatical year. My interest in American culture, in the changing American university, and in the undergraduate student culminated in a research proposal to study, as a freshman, at my own university. The research questions I formulated were general: What is the current culture at AnyU (my pseudonym for my university) as an example of the American public university? How do contemporary American students understand their education, and what do they want from it? How do they negotiate university life? What does college really teach?

I am not the first to undertake such a project. Michael Moffatt, also an anthropologist and a professor, wrote a valuable ethnography of undergraduate life at Rutgers University, which I often incorporate in my American culture course. In many ways it served as a historical reference point for what I witnessed in 2002–3. Moffatt conducted his fieldwork between 1977 and 1987, with literally a different generation of students, and his accounts—along with other important literature, such as Helen Lefkowitz Horowitz's history of campus life and Dorothy Holland and Margaret Eisenhart's investigation of women in college—provided me with a helpful foundation for assessing change and continuity in student culture.[3]

I thought, too, that I might bring a new slant to earlier work. As a woman, I expected that my purview would be decidedly different from Moffatt's male gaze on college life, with its heavy emphasis on sexuality. As a reader, you will find that some topics, such as Greek life, dating and sexuality, parents and students, commuters, and athletics, receive short shrift.[4] It is not that these subjects are unimportant to undergraduate culture; rather, I highlight topics that engage the classic notions we have of "the university" as a world of ideas, as a residential place where diversity and community and integrity are nurtured. I wanted to see how student culture articulates with the *institution* of the American university, including the vision we have of it, its mission, and its future.

To do this, I draw more heavily on the "participant" in participant-observer research than in earlier ethnography, where researchers, though they similarly relied on student interviews and observations for their data, were self-identified as professors.[5] I opted for a more daily immersion, in which I actually took courses, lived in the dorms, and encountered students as an older but fellow student.

In the spring of 2002 I applied to my own university as a student with an undeclared major, using only my high school transcripts as evidence of my education. I was accepted shortly afterward and began receiving "Welcome to AnyU" letters with information packets about financing my education, meal plans, and dormitory living, the summer "Previews" program that all freshmen were required to attend, and optional summer rafting and hiking trips I might want to join before school started.

After some reflection about my options, I decided it was best to "get with the program," following as closely as I could the student script for the first year. I opted, as most freshmen do, for a campus meal plan and on-campus dormitory housing; I signed up for a centrally located coed dormitory, consisting mostly of nineteen- and twenty-year-olds, although I requested and received a single room on my floor.[6] I sent in my forms to attend the two-day Previews session, where freshmen arrive—usually with their parents—to receive an orientation to college life prior to the start of classes. I also planned to arrive on campus a week before classes began to participate in "Welcome Week" activities for new and returning students. After hesitantly peeling my faculty parking sticker off my car and shelving my faculty ID, I prepared to enter my new status as a first-year student.

How I Would Represent Myself

The undergraduate application process, with its requirement that I list all schools attended and degrees received,[7] had begun a delicate balancing act between truth and fiction about my life. It was clear to me that if I entered student life announcing that I was a professor, I would compromise some of my purpose in doing this project. I wanted to see what college life was like as a student, albeit a "returning"[8] older student, and to relate to other students and to faculty members as a student rather than as a professor and researcher. At the same time, my commitment as an anthropologist is to refrain from misrepresenting myself to the people within the culture I am studying.

My friends and colleagues helped me wrestle with my problem of identity, asking, "What will you say if someone asks you what you do for a living?"

"Can't I say I'm not working now—that I'm a student?" I responded, thinking that this was true even if it wasn't the whole truth.

"Yes," a colleague agreed, "but what if they ask what you did before?"

"I'll tell them I've done many things—which I have. I can say that I'm a writer, among other things, because I still get royalties from my last book."

"But what if they say, 'What other things?'" one colleague pressed.

"Well, I hope they don't ask me that, but I guess I'd have to tell them that I teach and do research."

Friends, role-playing as students, continually engaged me in mock dialogues: So what's your major? "I'm undeclared." What's your hometown? "I was born and bred in New York." Why did you come to AnyU? "I wanted to see what college was like, because I'm a writer as well as a student, and this university was close to home. Besides, I love the town, the mountains, the outdoors here." All true, I reasoned.

As it turned out, my exercises in identity were largely moot. In daily conversations no one (with one exception, to whom I spilled all) ever asked me directly about my life. Two student friends confided to me later that they thought it was a little sad for an older woman like myself to be living in the dorms, and didn't want to ask me questions for fear that there was a horrific divorce story attached.

In formal interviews I always kept strictly to research protocol. I identified myself as a researcher doing a project on undergraduate life who intended to publish her results. I provided informants with a written description of the project and its goals, and asked for their signed permission to conduct an interview. Many of my informants also knew me as a fellow student, though, and I suspect that they thought my research goals and my intentions to publish my results were a combination of wishful thinking and academic bravado. I discuss the ramifications of disclosure and identity on my research in the afterword, "Ethics and Ethnography."

Enter the Abyss

My first real immersion in student life came in June of 2002, when I attended summer Previews, required for all incoming freshmen. Previews was an intensive two-day event that included an overnight stay at one of the premier freshman dorms. Freshmen were told to provide a sleeping bag, towel, and pillow for their dorm room, where they would be housed with another freshman. Bedding was provided for parents, who were to sleep in different wings of the same building.

I arrived at 8 AM to register outside the lobby of the large freshman dorm. I had thought carefully about how I would dress, and I showed up "consciously casual" in denim shorts and a golf shirt, baseball cap (bring a hat, we were advised), athletic socks, and not-too-new sneakers. Like the other freshmen, I carried my sleeping bag and pillow and overnight bag awkwardly as I stood in line waiting to get my key and my roommate assignment. "Excuse me, ma'am," said the blond ponytailed upperclassman working the intake desk, "parents go over there." She pointed. "No," I answered with an understanding smile. "I'm not a parent, I'm a freshman." I looked in the direction of her finger to see a group of waiting parents in the lobby, more than half of them wearing denim or athletic shorts, a collared golf-type shirt, baseball cap, and sneakers with athletic socks. The students wore flip-flops, jeans, and short T-shirts. It was already clear that my cultural acumen was flawed.

"Oh, I'm so sorry," she said. "That's so cool that you're coming to Previews! Well, then, you'll be rooming with Jennifer," and she pointed to the similarly blond ponytailed woman in front of me in line, who turned out to be a prospective health sciences major from Houston. I saw a look of what I considered to be controlled panic cross her face, but she quickly recovered to give me a smile and a greeting. I did feel bad for this poor freshman who drew the old lady for her first roommate, but I found that we could carry on a reasonable conversation about our majors, why we picked AnyU, and the two-day program.

During the next two days I discovered a number of things I never knew about my university. I attended information sessions on meal plans, registering for classes, how to get tutoring and advising help, different tuition payment options, and how to budget our time. There was a walking mall of tables for new students, highlighting services and groups on campus. As a new student, I was overwhelmed; as a professor, I was surprised to see how three particular spheres—sororities and fraternities, religious organizations, and commercial services, including credit cards and phone services—dominated the scene and vied for student attention. As an anthropologist, I was humbled to see how little I, as a professor, knew of my students' academic world.

Besides informational sessions, which parents and students attended together, the formal Previews program offered a number of icebreakers, upperclassman skits, and discussion sessions attended just by students. I stood in circles of students where we threw beanbags and learned individual names by calling the name of the person to whom we tossed the bag. We watched numerous cautionary student skits—on AIDS, on date rape, on drinking—and were asked to reflect on a number of social circumstances we might encounter in school: What if you had a gay roommate who put a pink triangle on the door? Which scenario did you think was worse, a wheelchair-bound student denied access to a second-floor dorm room or an African American student always being asked by the teacher to tell the class what blacks think?

Despite the great variety of planned activities, there was a curious sameness to many of them. As an anthropologist, I saw a "script" in these introductory experiences. First we were confronted with a controversial, usually emotionally engaging issue. Then we were asked, often in a small group, to reflect on what we thought about the issue or what we personally would do in those circumstances. Group leaders expected us to express our thoughts individually on the matter at hand, with the reminder to the group that "everyone is entitled to their view." The upshot was that the group listened politely while all of us, no matter what thought we voiced, shared our opinions. The exercise ended, without dialogue or interaction, when the last person had spoken. In this style of intellectual discourse I noticed some of the themes I would encounter throughout my undergraduate experience. More important, I could begin to see the repeated (and, after a while, anticipatable) elements of the experience that marked shared understandings and cultural elements.

Welcome Week: Life in Another Culture

I moved into my dorm room on a Saturday in August, the first day that students were allowed to take possession of their rooms. The following week was designated "Welcome Week," a time when students participate in optional social, sports, and orientation activities prior to the start of classes. Printed calendars of events, along with informal flyers, posters that hung from the lobby rafters, and tiny strips of paper that appeared regularly under my door announced a plethora of dorm events and university activities that competed for student attention.

The calendar for Welcome Week was listed by the hour— touch football game on the quad at 2; time management workshop on north campus at 3:30; an ice cream social at 7 in the dorm lobby—and there were RAs (resident assistants) reminding residents of the next activity and urging them to join in. The resident assistants had been on campus for more than a week preparing for the new students, making posters, designing dorm activities, and crafting decorative name tags for each resident's door. RAs were upperclassmen who received free room and board and a stipend to serve as peer counselors for a given wing or floor as well as local law enforcers for the residence halls. During this introductory week, they served as cheerleaders, encouraging incoming students to "get involved," and were the only people who knew our names: "Rebekah, will you be coming to the ice cream social?" "Hey, Rebekah, don't forget the movie tonight—free popcorn!"

The schedule was designed so that new students would choose from various activities, meet new people, and learn to negotiate the college campus. I joined as many activities as I could. As I began Welcome Week, I knew that I had started formal "fieldwork," but I had never quite anticipated how similar my entrance into college life would seem to my prior fieldwork in a remote village.

As a full-time faculty member for fourteen years, as well as a member of the faculty senate and other campus-wide organizations, I thought I was thoroughly familiar with my home institution. I knew all the shortcuts, both geographically and bureaucratically, for negotiating the campus and was completely comfortable with that knowledge. It came as a surprise, then, to discover after moving into the dorms that I was completely disoriented, much as when I arrived in the village where I first did my overseas fieldwork.

Our first week's calendar called for freshmen to attend a number of events all across campus. The campus, though, had taken on an entirely new physical appearance to me. As a professor, I was used to having my classes built around my *own* location, usually in or close to the anthropology building on the southern end of campus. When I needed to cross campus, I was accustomed to traveling by car—from faculty parking lot to faculty parking lot. I always entered buildings by the door closest to the parking lot and had a sort of "street-eye" view of the campus world.

Many campus buildings have a "street side" and a "walking mall" side. The mall side offers grassy areas and trees, benches with a few picnic tables, as well as walking and bicycle paths. As a student, I had a student parking permit. I was allowed to park in only one area of campus, near my dorm, and then had to walk or use the campus bus system to get to other areas of campus. From my new purview, the buildings and general geography looked completely different to me, so much so that I could not tell exactly where I was on campus, much less identify the building or door I was supposed to find. I could not locate the bookstore or the health clinic or the international student office, all buildings I thought I knew. Moreover, I was being asked to find offices and buildings I wasn't used to finding: the garage from which to get your rented refrigerator; the freshman advising office; the seminar room of the Hotel and Restaurant Management School. This was not my home turf.

I became one of many freshmen whom upperclassmen answered with patience: "Take the 3 Bus and get off at the Union." Or "Follow the walking path to the end and the building is on the left." I was shocked at how vulnerable and out of my element I felt. I found myself frequently wandering in the wrong direction and stopping other students, who looked more competent, for directions. I genuinely felt the part of a new student, or at least a clueless outsider.

My sense of cluelessness reached a peak on my second night in the dorm. I had just finished a dorm volleyball game played in the afternoon sun, and I was hot, thirsty, and hungry in that order. I showered in one of the four stalls provided for the seventy women on the floor, made myself a quick stir-fry in the first-floor communal kitchen, and broke open a cold beer from my rented mini-refrigerator. I brought my meal and drink into the second-floor lounge, putting both on one of the two round tables in the room.

I proceeded to eat and drink, as I watched CNN, and as other students—including my RA—wandered in and out of the lounge. About ten minutes into my meal, the lounge door burst open and, in what seemed a storm trooper–style raid, four RAs descended on me. "Do you realize that you cannot have alcoholic beverages in here?" the head RA demanded gruffly.

"No, I'm so sorry," I stammered. "I thought that this dorm allowed alcohol."

"Please give me your ID," she ordered, and as she wrote down my name and student ID number on a pad, she explained that residents may drink in the dorms if they're over twenty-one but not in public areas. You must be in your own room with the door closed. This was all in my student handbook, which I'd been given earlier in the week and should have read, and even if I hadn't, I was responsible for knowing what was in it. They would get back to me about disciplinary measures.

However embarrassed I was to be cited within forty-eight hours of starting the semester, my RA raid was curiously reminiscent of a famous ethnographic incident, and it buoyed my spirits. The incident occurred in Bali, where the anthropologist Clifford Geertz found himself running from the scene of an illegal cockfight that was raided by the police, scattering and hiding with other attendees. In Geertz's case, this proved to be his entrée into a community that had been wary of his presence: the villagers finally trusted him when they saw him running too. I hoped my drinking debacle would serve the same function for me.

There were other unexpected elements as well that reminded me of doing overseas fieldwork. One of these was language. In her study of student language, Connie Eble (1996) found that in a seven-year span (1980–87), only 10 percent of a college slang lexicon remained in use, and over fifteen years (1972–87), only four out of two hundred words stayed the same. I saw very quickly from the banter of the first week that I did not have my lingo straight, and that to increase rapport, I would have to master the current speech conventions. "Hooked up," for example, was a rough equivalent of 1970s "shacked up," and certain expressions were liberally peppered throughout most conversations, including "sweet," "lame," "awesome," "oh my god! oh my god!" "like" (e.g., "If I was to . . . like . . . go to class, I would . . . like . . . fall asleep"), and "totally!" among many others. These particular terms would likely change again within a few years, but for now they were important badges of in-group identity.[9]

There was also the speed of conversation. I didn't notice it much when a dorm mate spoke directly to me, but I found that when I was listening at the fringes of an interacting group, I sometimes had to strain to understand the conversation. It was as if they were using a different dialect of English—the way an American might feel overhearing a group of Welshmen speaking English informally. You sort of understand, but you can't catch every word. I often wished I had a transcript of the conversations that went by me in the dorms. The dialogue was so much faster than what I was used to speaking or hearing, and interestingly, it was quite a different speech style from my conversations with students as a professor.

As had been the case in my overseas world, sports played a positive role in my social acceptance into the dorm. In the first weeks of fieldwork, before I could speak much of the local language, life was very lonely in the village. When you can speak only a few words of a language, people tend to limit their interactions with you or treat you as a mental defective. Then I discovered that there was a Ping-Pong table at the local rectory and a regular contingent of teens to thirty-year-olds who showed up to play. I have always been a good athlete, and it was through Ping-Pong that I made my first friends and impressions; it provided one of the few venues where I could show my intelligence, through strategy or cleverness, or where we could share the emotion of a heated rally or close miss. Villagers saw me as a person when I played with them, as opposed to when I talked with them.

Touch football and volleyball played a similar role in my first week in the dorms. That I played at all, at five foot two, 115 pounds, and fifty-plus years, surprised the RAs and my hall mates. That I caught three passes helped cut through the stereotypes of the "older female student." I noticed more joking with me afterward. RAs made a point of telling me when an informal game of something or other was being organized outside. One student invited me to come to the new intramural rugby club for women. (I declined, fearing for my life, but appreciated the invitation.) Others had a new basis for saying a word or two to me in the hall, and vice versa.

I was feeling pretty good about my first whirlwind week of activities in school and the possibilities for full acceptance on my hall. I was acclimating well, I thought, to the late-night hours of the dorm and the loud chatter of conversation and music that permeated the halls. It was about midnight, almost a week after I moved into the dorm, and I was sitting in my room at my computer in pajamas with my back to my open door. A woman's voice came from behind me: "Excuse me, I'm looking for room 443. Can you tell me which direction?" I turned around to help her, now proudly familiar with the layout of my dorm, and she blurted, "Oh . . . sorry! I didn't know you were a mom," and proceeded to walk to the next open door.

That incident presaged a number of similar "mom" occasions, when people assumed in bizarre situations (such as at an underground rock concert or as I was walking out of class with a backpack on and pen in hand) that I was the mother of the person next to me. My old age assigned me to a niche, just as my nationality and young age had caused villagers where I once worked as an anthropologist to see me as a "Peace Corps."

No matter how good my local language skills became and how comfortable I was in my own resident village, I was always a Peace Corps worker to natives new or distant to me. The same proved true in the dorms. While I found that I felt close to being an equal in hands-on task situations—class projects, study groups, or sports—social situations were quite another story. To the students I didn't know well, including most of the men and women on my dorm floor, I was a very much older woman who, despite getting busted for drinking, was never really one of them.

My student life lasted an academic year, and the mainstay of this book is based on my participation in and observation of undergraduate life—both my own and others'—over the course of that year. Let me be clear about one thing, though. My personal experiences as a middle-aged woman cannot say anything directly about "the undergraduate experience." I am not eighteen years old, not subject to the same pushes and pulls of that age group nor privy to their social interactions. As anthropologists learn in their overseas experience, one can never really "go native" or expect that one's own experience is indicative of the experience of others born in the culture. At the same time, it is the experience of living village life that offers the insight and vantage point needed to ask relevant questions and understand the context of the answers given. It is this that I hoped to accomplish by becoming a freshman.

The pages that follow are informed by several types of data. In addition to national education studies and local surveys at my own university, I conducted forty formal interviews with American and international students, two focus groups (one with freshmen and one with seniors), and several "ministudies," including activity diaries completed by students about the use of their time, a five-month monitoring study of who (based on gender and perceived ethnicity) eats with whom in the student dining areas, a study of residential mobility, a descriptive weekly diary of all formal program activities conducted in my dorm, and a survey of informal conversation topics.

As a participant-observer I concentrated, as many freshmen do in their first semester, on learning the ropes, meeting other students, getting acclimated to the dorm, trying out student clubs, and discovering what it took to do my academic work. I spent every day and night of the week at the dorm, taking a full load of five undergraduate courses that ranged across the curriculum. Like other students, I went "home" only on the occasional weekend night or during holidays. I consciously chose a wide variety of courses, from modern languages to business and engineering, and professors whom I did not personally know (figuring that, if I didn't know them, they would not know me). My name appeared on the roster as that of a first-year student who had not yet decided on a major.

As most fieldworkers would do when starting a field project, I began by mapping the physical space of the dorm and did a "census" of my dorm wing. I listed all the public notices, advertisements, and flyers that were officially posted on the walls and bathroom stalls and noted the sayings, objects, and pictures that adorned individual dorm room doors facing public space. I kept descriptive records of dorm meetings, events, and incidents, as well as daily fieldnotes about my personal experiences, observations, and conversations.

During the second semester, when I was more actively engaged in formal student interviews and mini-study observations, I quietly dropped my class load down to two courses to accommodate my active research agenda, and spent several nights per week at my home computer, showing up back at the dorm most days after my early morning class. During both semesters I was the floor volunteer responsible for "graffiti questions" in the women's bathrooms, a sort of college female convention whereby a question is posted in each toilet stall with blank paper and a pen. The bathroom users respond anonymously, often posing new questions, and writing retorts to one another's responses. This became a constant source of comment and interaction about student issues and interests.

This book has the ambitious goal of describing "the undergraduate experience." In a strictly statistical sense this is impossible, because no school will be representative of all others, and even at one school no set of experiences or interviews can stand exactly for all others. At last count, in fact, there were more than 4,100 accredited institutions of higher learning leading to the bachelor's degree in the United States, and considerable variety within that educational pool. Given this diversity, what can one person's experience and research at a single school say about undergraduate life?

For one thing, AnyU, a public university with more than ten thousand students, is probably a reasonable representative of the places where most U.S. college students go to school. While the big university represents only 11 percent of the campuses across the country, it enrolls 51 percent of all college students.[10] Like most institutions in this "Big U" category, AnyU is a public doctoral-granting university offering a full spectrum of undergraduate majors and a respectable education at relatively reasonable cost. You would not find it listed in the top tiers of *U.S. News and World Report*'s "Best Universities," and as a non-elite state university, it draws its student body predominantly, but not exclusively, from within the state.

Still, AnyU's reputation for undergraduate education—including the presence of professors (not graduate students) in the classroom, a residential campus, and smaller-than-usual classes for a Big U—attracts a formidable pool of freshmen, the majority of whom ranked in the top quarter of their high school class. AnyU therefore seems solidly in the middle of the American college system, and should be familiar to many U.S. college students, though not identical to their experience.[11]

In making the case for AnyU, I also want to speak to you, the reader, as an anthropologist would. Anthropologists believe that the very nature of a culture is that it is something both learned and shared by others. Any person in my overseas village could tell you when it was time to plant, just as any American could tell you that you should stand up for the national anthem. Although many aspects of culture are contested—Should abortion be legal? Should English be the official U.S. language? Should gay people marry?—the conflict itself is often a recognizable aspect of the cultural scene. Because of this, I can write an entire book centering on one family from one village undergoing change, yet find that many other people from that country (several of whom have written me) recognize their own stories in its pages.

The same is true of the American public college. Even though colleges vary widely in their missions and student bodies, almost any American college student should be able to confirm that many students regularly sleep until noon or later, that classmates typically try to avoid Friday classes, that the first row in a lecture hall will fill up last, or that underage students drink secretly. Granted there are some students who get up early, a few who prefer the first row or who do not drink while they are underage, but these are cultural actors too, who are probably aware that they are contesting or flouting norms.

It is through the intimate and everyday experiences of college—revealed to me through interviews and participant-observation—that I aim to describe college culture. I contextualize what I see and comment on its content from several vantage points, including my outlook as a professor, the views of foreign students, and the insights provided by national surveys of college life. But the ultimate test of my analysis will be undergraduate students, who can decide for themselves if they recognize their lives and their world in this book.

CHAPTER 2

Life in the Dorms

Walking down the dorm corridor to find my room for the first time, I was struck most by the sheer amount of "stuff." Rooms and corridors were piled high with clothes, appliances, bedding, furniture, and countless boxes. As the clutter cleared during the day and rooms assumed their final appearance, it was hard to believe how many things had been squeezed into a ten-by-twenty-foot space.

I had personally made several shopping trips to stock my dorm room, and had moved in a few carloads of items, but my room—with its computer, lamp, night table, ten-inch TV, microwave oven, wok, books, comforter, and two posters—was bare compared with those of my younger compatriots. In addition to articles like mine, they had joysticks, couches, mountain bikes, ski and sports equipment, guitars and keyboards, large and elaborate sound systems, multiple-layered electronics shelves holding TVs, VCRs, DVD players, refrigerators, tables, cabinets, floor and pole lamps, overstuffed throw pillows, as well as coffeemakers, slow cookers, and illegal sandwich grills. What's more, many rooms had duplicates of every appliance—dueling computers, TV sets, microwave ovens, stereo systems.

Each room contained two single beds, a small sink and mirror, a large built-in armoire, and a double desk running the width of the room with multiple drawers and bookshelves, but almost all residents added creatively to the available storage space. There were hooks to hold bicycles that couldn't be left outside and under-the-bed containers for extra clothing. Some students bunked their beds to create space for their couches, beanbag chairs, electronics, and appliances; others placed their desk chairs on top of their desks to create floor space (I saw some do their homework up there as well). The rooms, built in the 1940s, literally could not hold all the items brought, and many residents built storage structures upward from floor to ceiling. Among the biggest differences in dorm room arrangement from my youth were lofts—elaborate wood frames that held a second-story platform over one's bed, creating another level of living and storage space.

Two people shared most rooms, with a few singles thrown in here and there. The geography, like the community, began with one's immediate wing, and then extended to one's corridor, floor, and finally dorm. The largest public spaces were on the ground floor and were communal for the entire dorm. A large lobby area with fireplace, lounge furniture, and television set greeted residents, with student newspapers, coupons, pizza delivery flyers, and activity calendars spread on a table for the taking. Depending on the day and the hour, student workers or resident assistants (RAs) staffed the front desk and were available from 8 AM to 10 PM for questions, problems, emergencies, and lending requests from the small video library. On this floor, too, there was a small communal kitchen, with a single stove, which served the entire building, as well as a computer lab open only at night and an exercise room, each the size of two dorm rooms.

My floor consisted of two contiguous male and female halls with a shared coed lounge area in between that housed a TV with VCR (but no DVD), two round tables with chairs, and a few overstuffed couches and chairs. The two female wings on each floor shared a same-sex bathroom, and the two male wings shared a second common bathroom. The female wings were slightly more populous, so approximately seventy women used four toilet stalls, four showers, and one bathtub.

Most mornings, before the start of popular 9–10 AM classes, there would be a line of women in bathrobes carrying plastic shower caddies with soap and shampoo, waiting for an open shower.

Resident assistants' rooms or suites were positioned strategically in high-traffic areas. There were three on my floor. You could tell their rooms by the animated decorations on their doors and wall spaces around their rooms. You might see a giant brightly colored name tag, a "Good luck with classes!" banner, or a door wrapped like a package, with a "Come on In" sign. The RA usually provided some way of knowing where he or she was at all times, with pointers indicating "eating out," "in class," "out and about," "studying—only emergencies," or "I'm there—knock." RA spaces, always busy with displays and messages, conveyed a kind of big brother or big sister authority, a mixture of law enforcement and availability, concern, and counsel.

Are We Having Fun Yet?

As I would do if I had moved into a village, I started my research by recording my immediate surroundings and taking a census of who lived where. There was a lot to record. Dorm doors, hallways, and bathrooms were filled with messages in the form of flyers, jokes, bulletin board displays, photos, and collages, all in their own way telling me something about the culture of the dorm.

Bulletin boards provided the official imagery of dorm life. There were several on each floor, and creating the displays was an important part of the RA's job. They were usually changed each month, so in a year's time one could see a healthy sample of topics and presentations. I typically wandered the halls on weekend mornings when they were reliably deserted because students were either sleeping or had left on Friday for a weekend adventure. By April of my second semester, I had recorded fifty-seven different formal bulletin board displays in my residence hall.[1]

It was clear that the bulletin boards were coordinated efforts, influenced by directives from the RHD (residence hall director); they rotated in a discernible pattern relating to the time of year and desired theme, although RAs had considerable leeway in deciding how a message appeared. At the beginning of the year the corridors all sported "get involved" messages as well as rape and sexual assault warnings. Mid-semester messages contained more academic advice but also focused on conflict resolution, roommate, and relationship problems. Around the December holidays, health and body image messages were more frequent, while around Valentine's Day was a profusion of boards relating to love, sex, and relationships. "Diversity" issues seemed relegated to the weeks surrounding the Martin Luther King Jr. holiday. I saw one board on voting preceding November elections.

Approximately one in five bulletin boards throughout the year concerned academics, and most of these offered tips and tools, including items such as "dealing with test anxiety" or "ten steps to academic success." The biggest category of displays—more than one-quarter—dealt with psychological and physical health, as well as threats to health. This category included four displays on sexual assault and sexually transmitted diseases, three on drugs and alcohol, and four on body image (for example, "Love your Lumps," urging us to accept our bodily imperfections).

Scattered comic relief boards that drew on college culture themes ("Fifty Things Admissions Never Told You about College," "Crazy Things to Do for under $10," "Fifty Fun Things to Do at Wal-Mart") appeared throughout the year. Almost 20 percent of all messages had danger motifs, warning students about the consequences (suspension/expulsion, AIDS, jail, STDs, pregnancy, sickness, even death) that given actions would reap. In visiting the dorm the following year, I found that many of the boards were recycled, suggesting that this formal culture—touting health, educational and academic advice, information, and warnings—had some consistency over time.

Resident doors, by contrast, belonged to the informal student culture. Although RAs had affixed a handmade name tag and welcome materials to each of our doors, I quickly learned that cool students added things and, boys in particular, took RA items down. Within three weeks of moving in, 60 percent of the boys' doors had been stripped of their RA materials. It was women, though, at about a 3 to 1 ratio to men, who had designed new, often elaborate door displays.

Although not all students of either gender decorated their doors, expressive door art was a regular feature of college life. A variety of objects, text, drawings, photos, collages, pictures, quotes, comic strips, and symbols—often ten to twenty or more on a single door—appeared as public yet personal door displays. If you were to ask students directly about the rules and meaning of door decoration, they would likely say that there are no rules (except for avoiding racial and ethnic slurs) and that door displays don't "mean" anything beyond the interests of the occupant. An anthropologist, though, would say that there are very particular rules and patterns that define the expressive culture of undergraduates, and the way students choose to represent themselves to others is very telling.

If the formal culture stressed advice, academics, and warnings, informal culture stressed sociability, fun, and humor. "Friendly fun," as Michael Moffatt found at Rutgers University, was "the bread and butter of college life."[2] In 2003, "fun" continued to be one of the most ubiquitous words in college discourse, a way to describe a good evening, a good person, or a good class. "Fun," as a concept, is associated with spontaneity, sociability, laughter, and behavior (including sexuality) that is unconstrained. The value placed on fun was evident in many forms on student doors, in the images and words that were selected for public viewing.

Probably the most common door display included strings of phrases and words cut from magazines, usually interspersed with cutout images. Although some doors posted discrete messages such as "Saying of the Week" or "Quotable Quotes," most used a collage-like genre to create a carefully constructed impression of freethinking spontaneity and individuality. On one representative door on my hall were the following phrases:

> Friends don't let friends party naked; Bitch; 24 hours in a day. 24 bottles of beer in a case. Coincidence? I think Not; Z-Man!! We Test Animals; Crazy Wild; Where the Stars Go; How Long Should you Wait?

While this reads on one level like a highly individualized, almost stream-of-consciousness expression, it is actually highly stylized. Its cutout words and phrases, set at different angles and using different sizes and fonts of type, were in the same visual style that appeared on most doors. Its content references to booze, nakedness, craziness, youth, celebrity, and sexuality were also common themes, which conveyed even larger themes of freedom and fun. Thus, down the hall on a neighboring door, one could see different phrases, also in pasted cutouts, that were manifestations of the same themes: "Bare your butt," "Young and Royal," "Las Vegas," "A Colorful Character," "Once Upon a Mattress," "The Next Best Thing to Naked," or on the next one "Welcome to CrazyWorld" and "Naked on Roller Skates."

Nudity, sexuality, drinking, craziness. These are certainly part of the college scene, but concentrating on the literal content alone misses the underlying values—fun, expressiveness, individuality, freedom, spontaneity—which are really the point. Images, like words, convey the same few themes. On one door it will be "nakedness" phrases that impart the impression of individuality, fun, a lack of limits; on another the same message is communicated with outdoor sport photos, showing a mountain biker or a skier in mid-air or a surfer riding a giant curling wave.

Acceptable alternative images or text include antiestablishment themes, in which the same core values of individuality and freedom are directed toward critique and rebellion. These door displays use dark, ghoulish, or frightening images: faces or bodies dripping with blood, Dracula-type/punk/goth images, skull and crossbones, a figure holding an automatic weapon. One such door with "dark" images displayed these verbal messages:

Swaying to the Rhythm of the New World Order; The Boogymen are Coming; Every time you Masturbate, God Kills a Kitten; Sort of; Korn Untouchables; Quit Smoking Later; The Rocky Horror Picture Show; Pay No Mind What Other Voices Say, they don't care about you.

Other acceptable messages are funny, cryptic, or eccentric, like this string of phrases on a single door: "Fight Club," "The Only Good Clown is a Dead Clown," and "Dream, Do you?" Although women and men share most of the expressive themes, friendship and love are, on the average, overrepresented on women's doors, while men's doors more frequently show images of violence, political critique, and humor, particularly in the form of cartoons.

Many of the implicit messages of dorm doors directly contradict those of the formal sector. Whereas careful forethought and the consideration of consequences are primary messages in the formal sector, informal student culture emphasizes spontaneity. Drinking, smoking, drugs, and sexuality, while commonly featured in warnings on bulletin boards and official postings, appear as objects of admiration on student doors. And while official messages wholeheartedly urge students to accept their bodies, the images on student doors are unambiguously young, lean, attractive, buff, and/or voluptuous. When fat, old, or unattractive people appear, they are almost always associated with ridicule and humor, thus reinforcing the inverse message.

Some of the most common images on student doors involve leisure and the "good life"—including martini glasses, palm trees, cowboys, guitars, flowers, bikinis, hearts, Hawaii, belly dancers, beaches. They offer an alternative to the "buckle down" vision of college in the formal sector, which implores students to apply themselves, to balance their social lives with study and seriousness of purpose. Among the diverse images I observed on student doors, none depicted books, studying, or academic honors—not even to critique them.

At least half of all pictures of people on student doors came from magazines or commercial posters, an indication that pop culture is a primary well from which students draw to construct their public identities. The range of "people images" typically included music, sports, and TV or film celebrities as well as anonymous sexy young men and women, models from ads who were either just "looking good" or engaged in an intense but "fun" activity: snowboarding, skiing, surfing, rock climbing, and cycling to name a few. Men, particularly but not exclusively, posted pictures depicting naked women, beauty queens, lesbian sexuality, and other sexualized women's images that were the objects of both comic and lustful gazes.

The images of "real" people—that is, photographs of the resident and people the resident knew—appeared on several doors, though less frequently than media images. With one exception, in hundreds of images there were no pictures of family members. Images that students chose for their doors were a particular genre of photograph that I can best describe with some examples (I cannot *show* them because of confidentiality requirements):

- The resident on a trip with a group of his friends. They all face the camera with arms outstretched in an "end-of-show" gesture, some on half-bended knees.
- A collage of photos taken during what clearly is a party. In one there are people wall-to-wall, as the resident holds up a glass in a toast.
- The two residents of the room, both making faces at the camera.
- A resident sticking her tongue out at the camera.

- Two residents of the room bending over and sticking out their rear ends (clad in jeans) at the camera.
- A mixed-gender group of friends on the ground, each person's head resting on the next person's stomach. The shot is taken from above, and everyone is laughing.
- The female resident and two girlfriends outdoors, facing the camera, with arms around one another's waist. The girl in the middle opens her mouth in mock surprise as the girls on either side point to her.

The images typically are not serious; they are often posed, but in poses that contrast with the family album picture. Instead of smiling naturally, people are often making faces, or purposely "over"-smiling, or sticking out their tongues. They appear in unusual positions (on the ground; with their butts sticking out) and/or off-balance, with legs and arms akimbo, as if caught in some spontaneous and "fun" activity. The photos almost exclusively feature the resident with others of the same age group.

Many of the photos—just as the words, phrases, and images included—are calculated to say something like: "Here I am doing crazy/spontaneous/'fun' things"; "Here I am having a good time with my friends"; or sometimes, "I'm a unique and eccentric individual." What makes door art, from phrases to images to photos, similar is the spirit and the values it conveys: friendliness, youth, freedom, sexiness, sociability, irreverence, fun, humor, intensity, eccentricity, lack of limits, spontaneity. These are the values of undergraduate life, and although there are many students who do not individually advance or emulate these values, they nonetheless serve as the cultural standard.[3]

The Absolutely Positively Mandatory First Hall Meeting

My first formal introductions to others on the corridor came in the form of a required corridor meeting, the first of the season.

A few days before, I happened on a group of hall mates in the lounge making signs for the meeting. In addition to advertising, as usual, that "pizza will be provided," the posters included urgent phrases such as "You MUST be there!" "Yes, we mean YOU!" "ABSOLUTELY MANDATORY MEETING."

"See you there," I said in passing, as one of the sign makers glanced up, but he responded that he wasn't looking forward to the meeting and might not go himself. He mocked: "Don't pee on the toilets, don't leave trash in the halls . . . I know what they're going to say. I don't need to hear it again."

"Yeah," said another sign maker to both of us, "but we wanna show support for our RA for the first meeting, so we probably *will* be there."

Not all corridor residents did show up, but the lounge still could not hold the fifty-plus men and women who arrived for the first meeting; the overflow sat in the doorways, draped themselves over the arms of couches, and squeezed into tiny open spots on the floor. As an icebreaker the RAs asked us to tell two things about ourselves that others would probably not know from meeting us. I was one of the first to go and mentioned that I had lived overseas in a remote place for a few years; others mentioned musical talents or double-jointedness, but most people reverted to departmental major, name, and hometown. No one ever asked me about the place where I'd lived or why I'd lived there.

After introductions we moved on to rules, such as "Don't take the screens out of your windows" and "Don't prop the outside doors open." Those of us with no roommate were directed to move all our things to one side of the room unless we had paid for a single room. This portion of the meeting was not terribly different from that envisioned by the sign makers. We were then asked what dorm activities we'd like to have this year, to a lackluster response.

Finally, the meeting turned to the subject of alcohol. Although I didn't openly take notes, the discussion went something like this. "If you're not twenty-one, you can't buy alcohol," the RA began.

"Hey, who on the floor is over twenty-one?" a resident asked to laughter as the "over twenty-ones" enthusiastically raised their hands to show the underage students who could buy liquor for them.

"Listen," said the male RA, "the RHD [residence hall director] is really serious about that—he'll turn you in to the police if it comes out that you bought liquor for anyone underage. But, hey, we're not here to bust your butt. We're not here to catch you at anything. So don't give us reason to. Like I said, if you're underage, it is illegal to drink, but if you're in your own room, and you've got your door shut, and you're not loud, and no one's getting sick—well, we have no reason to go in there. Get the message?"

We certainly did. This dual message was, I found, the primary way that student authority was expressed within college culture, and perhaps with the exception of those living in freshmen-only dorms, this speech was consistent with the experiences of most students. I also found the same pattern mentioned in literature about other universities.[4] "Bad" RAs enforced the letter of the law; "good" ones enforced what we students believed to be its spirit.

Besides RAs, the only authority figure ever mentioned in dorm meetings was the residence hall director, and a student saw the RHD only if there was a problem or an issue that needed handling. Unless one did something outrageous or unluckily public, most of student life flew under the radar of university-level authorities, whom, as in Moffatt's day, few students could even name. The deans, provosts, and vice presidents, so important to faculty, remained part of an amorphous university structure that had little to do with students unless they really bungled their lives. In college culture the rules are perceived to come from "outside," and it was the job of an astute college student to keep his or her real life private and "inside," certainly behind closed doors.

That first all-hall meeting would be the last dorm meeting that more than a handful of people attended—even the absolutely positively mandatory ones.

School Days

My first week of college, before classes began, fit my idealized sense of college life. There was a buzz of activity as we all unpacked and began putting our rooms and door displays together. I watched carefully, realizing that most students were hanging message boards outside their doors that could record greetings, questions, and invitations from others who came by to visit when they were out. I bought and hung my own message board, realizing that, like dorm doors generally, it too served as a symbol—of friendliness and perhaps, when filled with messages, one's popularity.

During the day, dorm room doors were left wide open, as people unpacked and rearranged, and there was an animated life to the halls. The sights and sounds on my corridor were most vibrant in the evenings: one girl rolling another in a laundry basket down the hall to accompanying peals of laughter; someone drunk and sick throwing up in the girls' bathroom; two guys skateboarding illegally in the corridor; a bass thumping from one of the boys' rooms that shook the entire corridor; and the continual beeps from the boys' hall of XBX video game players who had shot one of the enemy.

There was a stream of social activities—a movie; a game night; an ice cream social; a bonfire and concert on the square, which most of the RAs attended and actively solicited us to join. One night I was the official spinner for the lobby game of Twister, which we played until we couldn't determine a winner. On another night I joined a group watching a video in the RA's room, contributing my plate of oozing microwaved eggrolls to the bags of microwaved popcorn already popped for the occasion. Together, propped on floor pillows, we watched a video about a man who loses his wife, a doctor, in an accident and finds another, a waitress, who received his wife's heart in a transplant. Although I had never encountered this film anywhere, it was apparently a cherished standby for most in attendance, who had seen it multiple times.

I spent one fascinating evening that I didn't fully understand. For more than two hours I watched five students set up a scenario for a role-playing game, an exceedingly complex contemporary iteration of Dungeons and Dragons. Among the activities laid down by the game leader was a random name generator that, on one of its runs, put together "academic title" words into new combinations, generating results such as "theoretical psychological anthropologist," "applied philosophical mathematician," and "critical historical sociologist." While I was chuckling to myself that these weren't far from the jargon that academics invent, one of the students commented that "these titles are as bogus as what we are actually doing here," to murmurs of agreement.

Then classes started. The planned daily activities ended and RA attentiveness waned. People retreated to their own lives and insular social groups, and real dorm life, as I would come to know it, began.

The start of classes brought a whole new slate of contacts and relationships, and it also ushered in a new set of daily responsibilities and realities. To get a sense of the rhythms of people's lives, I did my best to observe carefully the comings and goings on my own hall. As schedules became more regularized, I had hoped to perceive the shape of undergraduate days and nights.

This proved an elusive task because of the nature of our lives as students. Bombarded with lists of books to get (or return) and first assignments, I found it hard enough to keep track of my own life, let alone the activities of numerous others. I began to feel as harried as my fellow students as I located my rescheduled classrooms, met my professors, and began feeling the pressing demands of homework. My daily journal included entries that reminded me of my high school diary, filled with anxieties about deadlines and frustrations over mundane events: "Had to return to the bookstore four times (!) because professors subtracted or added books!"; "Bought my day planner but no time to fill it in"; "Went to three different buildings before I found my freshman seminar class."

My hall mates were like ships that passed in the night, greeting one another cursorily as we came back and forth from classes. Dorm life continued to be friendly, and I regularly inquired, as did my fellow students, about hall mates' days and classes. "How was your first week of college?" one boyfriend of a neighbor asked in amusement as I walked down the hall.

"Overwhelming," I responded.

"It gets better," he assured me.

"Did anybody make it to all their classes?" someone else asked a group of four. Only one person admitted she did.

Somehow, though, I had expected students' lives to be more public, more like my first week in the dorms, and for students to be involved with dorm mates in a number of joint events. I found that much more of student life than I had initially thought occurred behind closed doors and was not amenable to my participation or observation. As I would realize later on, these initial experiences reflected more than methodological problems; they pointed, as will become clear in this chapter, to some central themes in contemporary college life.

It wasn't until my own life as a student had settled more, and I began to do interviews and collect time diaries from other students, that I would begin to notice the patterns and patterned variations in student life.[5] It took even longer still to understand the forces behind the patterns.

Some things about college life had probably not changed that much since the 1970s, when Moffatt initially collected data about students at Rutgers University. His student sample, like mine, slept about eight hours a day and attended classes or dealt with university bureaucracy about four hours per day during the week. In his data, two-thirds studied about two hours a day, 10 to 15 percent worked harder than that, and 25 percent studied hardly at all, usually cramming at exam time.[6]

National samples of students suggest that class preparation time in 2003 was about the same, or, if anything, had slightly eroded. Forty-five percent of seniors in the United States (and 43 percent of freshmen) reported spending between one and ten hours per seven-day week preparing for class—well under two hours a day—while 20 percent worked more than twenty hours (with 11 percent reporting more than twenty-five hours per week), and the rest somewhere in between.[7]

These statistics roughly jibe with my own student reports. In the twenty days of student diaries I collected, the median daily class preparation time was about an hour and forty-five minutes (two hours if you use the average), or twelve and a quarter hours per week, a figure that included studying, reading, doing research, and writing papers, as well as watching class videos and meeting with project groups. The variation from day to day, though, was notable. While one-third of the time, students put in one hour or less of daily course preparation, they put in four or more hours on one out of every five days.

So if students are studying a little less, are they relaxing and partying more? The answer, despite the rhetoric of student culture, is no. Moffatt's students relaxed and socialized an estimated four hours per day. Only 12 percent of seniors and 17 percent of freshmen in the 2003 National Survey of Student Engagement (NSSE) reported relaxing or socializing even *three* or more hours a day. Sixty percent of seniors nationwide, and 53 percent of freshmen, said that they relaxed or socialized between one and ten hours per week, decidedly less than two hours per day. Even if one assumes, as I do, that these national surveys—which ask students to reflect on an entire week and self-report—are flawed, I also saw a relative dearth of "down time" when I totaled the minutes spent in various activities from the more reliable daily diary logs. In my own hall sample, the median number of hours spent socializing or relaxing was 2.88 hours a day,[8] down considerably from Moffatt's observations in the 1970s and 1980s.

The data suggested then that, compared to students a couple of decades ago, today's public college students are both studying a little less and socializing less. What, then, are they doing with their "extra" time?

According to my local sample, students were first and foremost working jobs, both inside and outside the university.

Whereas Moffatt reported that one of eight of his sampled students was working, more than half of my sample had a wage-paying job, working from six to over twenty-five hours, with a median of fifteen hours, every week. The NSSE survey for 2003 confirmed the huge upswing in students at work nationwide, finding that 31 percent of freshmen and a whopping 56 percent of seniors held some kind of *off-campus* paying job. And many more students worked on campus. In total, two-thirds of all students were working, including 54 percent of first-year students and 88 percent of seniors. Nationally, full-time students worked an average of ten hours per week.

My AnyU sample called attention to some other changes in time use as well. Although extracurricular clubs and organizations were not a central focus of student activity in either Moffatt's study or my own,[9] my interviews with students about their extracurricular participation showed that about half of those in my sample were involved in professional clubs and in volunteer work. I mention these in the same breath because I learned from interviews that joining professional clubs and volunteering are related. As one junior, Kate, explained to me:

> As a freshman I joined the pre-vet club and then last year I joined my professional Honor Society, which meets every other Thursday. Both of them require community service hours—which it's really important to have for vet school. That's why we [the organization's membership] do volunteer hours and fundraisers for community causes—the group helps us to beef up our résumés, and this helps us professionally when we apply to schools.

Many students who spoke with me viewed clubs and community work with this same eye for career. In a group of thirteen students whom I had interviewed about club participation, six were currently members of a professional group, most requiring community service, while only two participated in sports groups, two at some level of student government or politics, and one in a religious group. Personal interest clubs were noticeably lacking. Although sports and fitness interests ran high, many in the sample had declined to join a group and instead worked out at the gym either individually or with a friend. Kyle had participated in a poetry slam group, Deb had joined a campus booster/guide program, and Kate had attended a karate club, but all had grown too busy to continue. It was these groups that were sacrificed in students' participation histories, with only one student maintaining a multiyear membership in a group focused on her personal interests.

For half of the six ethnic minorities in my interview sample, an ethnic-based club or professional organization was important in their lives, and although their degree of participation waned and waxed in some semesters, these groups were an enduring presence over their college career.

By listing and aggregating the activities named in students' daily diaries, one could see that only about fifty types of activities—which included eating, socializing, napping, walking to class, going on-line, watching TV and videos, working out, studying or doing homework, listening to music, playing video games, and attending meetings—accounted for most of what students do in a given week. Students typically "multitasked": many went on-line while they ate or chatted on the cell phone while walking to class or did homework while watching TV.

It might surprise parents to learn that on a typical weeknight, more than half of dorm residents were in bed by 11:30 PM, and most were up the next morning by 9 AM.[10] The real experience of "college life," though, was in the variation—the sense that it was also considered normal to stay up past 2 AM or to awaken after noon. One-quarter of the time, sampled hall mates stayed up after 1 AM (several after 3 AM), and 15 percent of the time, students slept past noon, even on a weekday. Thus, college culture included the comical and ubiquitous ringing of alarm clocks at 2:00 in the afternoon, just as it did an abiding tolerance for those whose schedules are the inverse of one's own.

A typical week was thus very different for different students. Whereas the ROTC students were up before 6 AM to fit in their training commitments, and kept their evening outings to a minimum, the sorority pledge was out late both nights recorded in her diary log and confided that because of sorority commitments, there were many weeks when she had four late nights of obligations. She slept in past noon when she could. The varsity runner on the floor could almost never attend an outside dorm or university event in the evening; between his classes, daily morning and evening workouts, and weekend track meets, the only time he could study was weekday evenings.

All ten of the students I followed closely had constructed lives so distinct that their paths would cross only with great effort. It is no wonder that I had difficulty discerning the rhythm of the typical student day, as you can see in just these brief portraits of four students on my hall.

Casey is up at 5 AM most days because of ROTC training, which she admits is the biggest part of her life. Despite this daily commitment, she also remains active in a professional club and a demanding multicultural leadership program. Casey dropped her meal plan because she no longer had time to eat, and adds that she thought about joining a sorority but felt that "if I added that to my plate, I couldn't finish it." What social life she has centers on other ROTC students, including her roommate, whose schedules have more in common with her own. She typically eats alone in her dorm room whenever there's a break—mostly ramen noodles and microwave food—and finds that she has to extend her day past the bedtime she'd like in order to finish studying.

Ossie's days are longer, too, but for different reasons. An ethnic minority like Casey, Ossie, by his own admission, has become a terrible procrastinator—more lax and relaxed than in high school days. "One of the reasons is that I'm not sure what I want to do," he says. "I've changed my major seven times." Because of this he has had to go to school in the summer to stay on track, and his biggest challenge in college is keeping up with classes. "I stay at the university because of my friends—if it wasn't for them I'd be at a different school." Ossie likes to get out and socialize at least three nights a week. As he describes it, "I also like to keep busy," so in addition to his school and social life, Ossie works over twenty-five hours a week, which provides money for food and his nights out. Ossie's schedule leaves no time for clubs or interest groups.

Cynthia shared a class with me which she regularly "ditched." It is a matter, she explains, of priorities. She is an art major, and very serious about her art, which takes up most of her time. In addition to her heavy studio schedule, Cynthia works——both on campus, at an office, and off campus, at a local bar. Between her classes, her art, and her jobs, there is little time for much else. She stopped her regular attendance at two student groups she had joined and admits, "I don't see friends a lot. My social life is my [bar] job." Aside from a close roommate from high school, the only other friends she sees are people in her art classes. She eats irregularly, by her admission, whenever she can fit it in, and so she passed on a meal ticket: "I have to remind myself, 'Don't forget to eat!'" She estimates that she gets only five or six hours of sleep because she doesn't start studying until 10 PM when she's not working in the bar.

As a committed Christian, Kyle has a well-rounded life that centers on a small but close set of friends who are deeply involved in his church. A good student, Kyle apportions part of every week day for studying. He has learned to treat school like a nine-to-five job, and between those hours he attends class and tries to fit in all his reading, papers, and preparation. This is purposeful so that nights and weekends are free for Kyle's social, church, and volunteer activities. With others in his circle, he volunteers at a food bank and visits the elderly two nights a week; he spends two out of every three weekends away at religious retreats or outreach programs. He has chosen to live with and close to other members of the Christian community, and they try to have an evening meal or tea with one another at least twice a week. Kyle has a meal ticket, as do some others of his group, and they often buy meals for those in their circle without a ticket so that they can all eat together.

On one level, the diverse student lifestyles described here are simply attributable to choices emanating from differences in individual agendas and personality. From a cultural standpoint, though, it is clear that while people everywhere are different, the social structures in which they live do not always give free rein to those differences. Daily college routines, and the huge variation in the shape of days from student to student, was really a manifestation of something deeper about the nature of the university. Beneath differences in daily routine was a set of decisions that students made, and underlying their decisions was a set of options built in to AnyU and in to the structure of the American university. Would the students major in A or B or Z? Go to Spanish class, section 1 or section 10? Would they live on campus or off? In dorm X or dorm Y? Would they sign up for a meal plan or eat in their room? Would they spend most weekends away? Would they get a job while they went to school? Do volunteer work? Join ROTC? Would they pledge a fraternity or sorority?

In many ways, the microcosm of my corridor explained much about my experience of college life, and about why the national cries for "community" in the American college go unanswered.[11] It is hard to create community when the sheer number of options in college life generate a system in which no one is in the same place at the same time.

This is less a feature of intentional academic policy than it is of the premium Americans place on individuality and choice coupled with basic mathematics. If one hundred people make one choice, such as dorm A or dorm B, then, assuming the options are equally attractive, fifty people will be dorm A mates while fifty will live together in dorm B. But say, then, that the same fifty people in each dorm choose from one of five majors and one of three meal plans. How many have made the same choices and are likely to be in the same dining area, dorm, and major classes? Just three of the original one hundred, and that takes into account only this limited range of options. If we allow people to choose from one hundred majors, and add in decisions like being in a fraternity, going out for a sport, or living off campus, we can see that even with the thousands of students at a state university, very few students will have created college paths that cross frequently. Even good friends who have chosen to live together will have different majors, different courses, different clubs, and jobs that define divergent paths in their day-to-day lives.

Two implications follow from what can be called our "over-optioned" public university system. The first is that there is little that is automatically shared among people by virtue of attending the same university. On a practical level, what this means is that friends won't normally take the same classes; classmates won't usually go home to the same dorm; and hall mates won't often eat together, because some have meal plans while others buy their own food. It thus takes forethought and effort to overlap with others or to build a social circle, and the people who "naturally" meet (i.e., by virtue of having the same commitments) are most likely to be those who are glaringly alike.

The second implication is that, despite the emphasis on community, one can easily opt to move out of the dorm, drop the class, change majors, or quit the club, resulting in a social world that always seems to be in flux. The university "community" becomes both elusive and unreliable. When I came back to visit my dorm the semester after I finished my project, I could not find one person on my old corridor whom I recognized. "What happened?" I asked incredulously when I found one familiar RA face on a different floor. "Everyone moved. I think there's only one person from last year still on your corridor." I had seen 10 percent of my dorm population change by the time my first semester ended and 25 percent by the third week of my second semester.[12] One year later it was clear that, at least in university housing, one could never "go home." I shouldn't have been so surprised, really, because in a system in which one can choose from a number of living arrangements at any time, people do choose, and choose again.

The same is true of most aspects of university life. Thus, in my very small sample, the majority of students I interviewed had had at least two different majors, switching from one to seven times. Most also had joined and left at least one organization or club, quitting because the organization no longer appealed to them or the meeting bumped heads with another, more important activity.

In this light, the university becomes, for individual students, an optional set of activities and a fluid set of people whose paths are ever-shifting. Seen from the level of the institution, "community" is a lofty ideal but with few common activities, rituals, or even symbols to bind together its diverse inhabitants. What little one might share with some other students—a major, a residence hall, an interest—is always in flux. How this plays out for two of the most touted values of university life, community and diversity, is the subject of the next chapter.

CHAPTER 3

Community and Diversity

O ne would be hard-pressed to find words more wide-spread in university rhetoric than "community" and "diversity." As a student, one is immediately enlisted to join the group, to get involved, to realize that one has become a part of the AnyU "community."

It starts during Previews and Welcome Week. We sing the AnyU alma mater with leaders; we learn the AnyU cheer. At the convocation that commences our freshman year, we are welcomed to AnyU with some statistics about our class, and then an entertaining PowerPoint presentation with voice-over begins: "In the year that you were born . . ."—it goes back eighteen years and shows a baby—"Ronald Reagan was president, AnyU was building its South Campus, and the movie that won the Academy Award was *Out of Africa*. We see graphics of all this, and AnyU history, at least for the past eighteen years, is interspersed with the shared "history" of the audience, which consists primarily of movies, TV shows, and dramatic historical events. "In 1986," the story continues, "the Emmy goes to *L.A. Law,* and the explosion of the *Challenger* saddens the American public." The presentation takes us briefly through all eighteen years of the baby-who-is-us.

By 1991 we have torn down the Berlin Wall, constructed the new AnyU library, and arrived at the same year that *Seinfeld* begins. There is silence, clapping, or booing as the event being described moves us. Our history continues, year by year, to mention, among other things, the end of the TV series *Cheers* in 1993, the Monica Lewinsky scandal in 1998, the beginning of *Friends* in 1994 (to thunderous applause), and the September 11, 2001, attack. By 2002 we are eighteen and ready to go to college, and—the lights come on—here we are, part of the AnyU family.

The presentation works; it is relatively short, and students leave mildly entertained and energized, having experienced a compressed version of our joint heritage and our shared place at the starting line of something new. It is clear what the common heritage has been constructed to be. What holds students together, really, is age, pop culture, a handful of (recent) historical events, and getting a degree. No one ever remembers the institutional history or the never-sung alma mater.

How Community Works at AnyU

Youth, pop culture, and getting a degree are pretty accurately the ties that bind together a public state university "community." Unless it offers a big-time (and winning) sports team that draws large attendance and loyalty, there is little in the way of shared first-year experiences that three thousand or so freshmen will have in common. AnyU did have a Freshman Colloquium course that was mandatory for all first-year students. It was designed to be just such a community builder, one that required students to complete a summer reading assignment— usually a provocative contemporary novel chosen collectively by the participating faculty—-that would be discussed in small seminars before classes formally began.

The faculty had an ambitious, and what they thought exciting, intellectual agenda in mind. Students would read the same book, and then their academic career would start with a stimulating seminar-style discussion with only twenty or so participants. The entire freshman class would be engaged in the same reading, and thus have a common basis for debate and dialogue. Freshmen would then meet the book's author, who had been invited at great expense to give a talk following their small-group discussions. This experience would jump-start the colloquium that would follow: a small, seminar-based freshman course centered on readings about community and citizenship, diversity, environment, and technology, designed to help them explore their journeys as "thinking persons," including the purpose of the liberal education they had begun. For the administration, the course was also a way to build a sense of loyalty and community, and thus, according to official belief, to retain freshmen as paying students.

I was in one of the last freshman classes to take the course. It was nullified as a requirement because the university faculty and administration concluded that it wasn't working. For one thing, only about a third of the students actually did the summer reading. My own pre-course seminar was led by an impressive instructor who practically pulled teeth trying to get a response to questions raised by our reading: "Does a common enemy help to make people a community? What is a typical American or an ideal citizen? Can anyone think of places within America that seem like a different country? Does technology bring you closer to or farther away from other people—does it separate or connect?" She ended up letting us go a half-hour early because, I surmised, of our silence. Very few in my seminar had read the book, at least "all the way through," as one student qualified it.

According to student surveys, many disliked the course that followed, in particular the idea that they "had no choice and that they *had* to take it," but also because it was abstract and impractical, and they didn't learn anything "related to their interests." The requirement, designed as the only common academic experience the freshmen would have, was accordingly wiped from the books, leaving an elective course, chosen separately by each student, in its place.

One can learn from the fate of the freshman seminar. It is a good example of what happens nowadays when efforts at building community compete with the demand for choice. The freshman course had been designed and initiated at AnyU as part of a nationwide agenda, begun in the early 1990s, to engage students in their freshman year and quickly establish a "learning community." It was one local response to what educational policy analysts identified as a crisis in community that left the university to be experienced in "momentary and marginal ways." "Not only has cultural coherence faded," reads the thoughtful and influential 1990 report from the Carnegie Foundation for the Advancement of Teaching, "but the very notion of commonalities seems strikingly inapplicable to the vigorous diversity of contemporary life." Titled *Campus Life: In Search of Community,* the report called for a renewal of community in higher learning. Its authors wrote:

> It is of special significance, we believe, that higher learning institutions, even the big, complex ones, continue to use the familiar rhetoric of "community" to describe campus life and even use the metaphor of "family." Especially significant, 97 percent of the college and university presidents we surveyed said they "strongly believe in the importance of community." Almost all the presidents agreed that "community is appropriate for my campus" and also support the proposition that "administrators should make a greater effort to strengthen common purposes and shared experiences."[1]

It is a cry that has been taken up in earnest by university presidents around the country. Because *requiring* common experiences is vastly unpopular, and efforts often meet the fate of the freshman seminar, AnyU, like many universities today, encourages community through elective participation. "If you don't see what you like," said one Welcome Week booster, "start your own club." The 158 registered student organizations on campus don't tell the full story of the options that confront a student in a single week, from salsa dancing night at a downtown club, to the regular pickup game of coed volleyball, to the Overeaters Anonymous meeting, to the self-defense lesson in the dorm, to the plethora of academic events that are part of lecture and film series.

Every week the hall bulletin boards are plastered with notices about new events to attend, new music groups in town, or organizations offering enthusiastic invitations to their open house. The proliferation of event choices, together with the consistent message to "get involved," and the ever available option of dropping out, creates a self-contradictory system. Students are confronted with an endless slate of activities vying for their time. Every decision not to join but to keep one's time for oneself is interpreted as "student apathy" or "program irrelevance," and ever more activities are designed to remedy them. Each decision to join something new pulls at another commitment, fragmenting the whole even further. Not only people but also community are spread thin.

In my life as a student this process of community building through elective involvement was repeated numerous times and in numerous places within the university. On my dorm floor alone, where we had not done much together as a group during my first semester, the process worked like this. To begin our second semester and usher in a renewed spirit of community, our enthusiastic RA devised an "interest survey," which she administered at the first mandatory hall meeting of that period. (Since it was second semester, the turnout was decidedly sparse: only six people attended.) "Let's do more things together," the RA suggested, and we agreed. It would be desirable, the collective thinking seemed to be, to have more "community" in the dorm.

"What would we like to do this semester?" she asked us. To find out, she distributed the survey with a written checklist that would assist her in launching new dorm programs that fit our interests and schedules. There were sixty-four activities suggested on the checklist in ten categories (community living, health/wellness, social awareness, employment skills, academic programs, relationship issues . . .), which ranged from presentation and panels, to group games and activities, to participatory workshops. We could write in activities if the ones presented did not suit. There was also an availability section of the form, where we were asked to check our preferred times—which evenings, which hours—for the activities. Because the showing at the meeting was so meager, our RA placed questionnaires under each of the doors on the wing, to be returned to her by a specified date. I asked whether I could see the final tallies.

A total of 304 selections were made by all hall mates, with eighteen of the sixty-four listed activities chosen by approximately half of all respondents. The most popular choice was not an activity at all but an expressed interest in buying floor T-shirts or boxer shorts. Among activities, several—including swing or salsa dancing and playing board games—were high on the list, but the RA decided to start her local "community" program with the biggest vote-getter, "Movie Night," endorsed by about three-quarters of the voting residents on the floor.

Movie Night was an activity whereby once every other week we would come to our RA's room, as in Welcome Week, to watch a movie on video while sharing popcorn and other snacks provided by the RA or anted up by the residents. The preferred time, according to the questionnaires, was 8 PM on Tuesday. And so Movie Night was instituted twice a month on Tuesday nights, and slips of paper appeared under our doors to announce the first movie. On the first Tuesday, two people showed, besides the RA. The second time nobody showed. The RA moved the night to Sunday. Still nobody showed. The program was canceled, leaving the RA wondering what she could do to "really involve" her corridor.

Two organizational levels up from the corridor was the dorm. Here RAs and dorm officers attempted more extensive full-dorm programs that would get the residents involved. There were dozens of them, in addition to the corridor or floor-level activities devised by individual RAs. The most residents I ever saw attend any single event in our dormitory, housing about four hundred people, was for the talent show, where there were about twenty-one people—mostly the talent—and the "How to Make Edible Underwear" program around Valentine's Day, which drew twenty-three people.

With varying degrees of success, this was the pattern of "community involvement" that operated at various levels of the university: a multiplicity of voluntary activities, a handful of participants at each, and renewed efforts to create new activities that were more relevant and attractive, resulting in an even greater proliferation of choices and fragmentation of the whole.

The American Way: The Individualism in Community

To university administrators my story of Movie Night would be yet one more example of failing involvement and community on the contemporary college campus. By 1990 it was already becoming clear that few students participate in campus events; 76 percent of college and university presidents called nonparticipation a moderate to major problem on campuses.[2] An RA might count Movie Night as a personal failure, and become dispirited by the apathy of residents, or perhaps hear a call to invent more and better activities.

Students, I imagine, would see it a little differently. The activities chosen were not the "wrong" ones, nor were their RAs remiss. Nor had students been insincere in their desire for more community life in the dorm. If you had asked most students what happened with Movie Night, they would have answered, "I wanted to go, but when the time came, I didn't," or "I forgot." They genuinely want to have a close community, while at the same time they resist the claims that community makes on their schedule and resources in the name of individualism, spontaneity, freedom, and choice.

This is exactly how many students talk about sororities and fraternities. Fewer than 10 percent of AnyU residents are members of either. When I asked students whether they'd considered "rushing," instead of mentioning the "elitism" or "conservative politics" that dominated Greek critique in my day, students complained about "conformity" and "control of my life." Judy explained that she had almost rushed but then changed her mind because "you become lost. It's hard to know all ninety girls in a sorority. You become the same rather than an individual in a group. It can get, you know, almost cult-like, and you spend all your time there. You can't live in other dorms, or meet new people."

I found that students' greatest objections to the Greek system were its steep demands—that it required so much time ("I can't give up that many nights a week to one organization") and so many resources ("Why should I pay all that money to a fraternity to have friends when I can make friends for free?"), all of them mandatory ("I don't want people telling me what to do and where I have to be all the time"; "I'm an individual, not a group person"). Yet, the one AnyU student in ten who did join a fraternity or sorority was, according to 2003 surveys conducted by the Office of Student Life, much less likely to drop out of school and much more likely to report the highest level of satisfaction with campus life.

There is a familiar dilemma here. "The very organizations that give security to students," concluded national policy analysts in 1990, "can also create isolation and even generate friction on the campus."[3] More than half of university presidents were reported to view Greek life as a problem, largely because it creates "little loyalties" that isolate students, removing them from the mainstream life of the university. It is not just Greek groups that operate this way. They are only illustrative of what one university president saw as "a great deal of 'orbital energy' among the many subgroups, a magnetism that tugs at these groups, pulling them away from any common agenda."[4]

Struggling with community in this way is, as observers of American life have pointed out, the American way.[5] The same things that make us feel connected and protected are the things that make us feel obligated and trapped as individuals and/or cut off from other groups with different agendas. For most students, as for most Americans in general, the "big community" has a dual connotation that includes both a warm and fuzzy

side, all about "oneness" or "togetherness" or "common purpose," and a negative side that tends to surface with reference
to government regulations, Big Brother images, and fears of
conformity. When students talk about their educational community, these contradictory ideas of community are reproduced, bouncing between an entity that provides love and a
sense of belonging and one that limits freedom and imposes
new obligations.

I initially encountered student thoughts about community
on "introduction sheets," tellingly titled "IT'S ALL ABOUT ME,"
that the RA had asked us to fill out and hang on our doors.
Aimed at "community building," the sheets posed questions
designed to acquaint others on the hall with our opinions and
personality. After blanks for our major, hometown, and favorite
color, and prompts to name our distinctive qualities, "the
things I like to do for fun," and "what makes you unique," was
the question, "What does community mean to you?"

For half the students, community was a somewhat naïve
amalgam of love, belonging, sharing, and togetherness—all the
things we would want community to do for us with none of its
obligations. It was, in their words, "respect; caring, open
people" who would be "sharing together, always there for me";
a place where there are "pillows on the floor" and "everybody
leaves their door open," where you can "crash on your neighbor's floor if you're too tired to go home." My favorite answer
in this category was "Community means being able to fart
comfortably," because it so perfectly ignores the possibility of
being the one at the other end of the farting freedom who has to
put up with her flatulent neighbors. Only one person, in fact,
mentioned any kind of responsibility when defining community, stating that she would "pick up garbage when I see it on
the ground."

The downside of the community coin was also well represented, with some students balking at the idea of community
or making jokes: "Community means Communism"; "Community means dirt—-do you realize how many germs infest

close-proximity living quarters?"; "Community means I can do whatever annoying habits I want and if my neighbors don't like it they can move out."

What I saw in student responses, as well as in student behavior, was a profound ambivalence about community life, resulting in a tentative, often conflicted relationship to the collective life of the university. Not only did campus participation suffer from this conflict, but also it was difficult to create mutual commitments and agreements among people whose connection to community was so hesitant.

One of the most interesting community ventures at AnyU came in the form of our second hall meeting in each semester, where we devised our "Community Living Agreement." Initiated by the RAs, these were to be the local agreements that each wing lived by, the "dos and don'ts" of hall life, fashioned by the residents themselves. The agreement for the first semester was drafted at a "mandatory" hall meeting at which seven people on the wing showed, one of whom left almost immediately because it was her birthday and she was too drunk to pay attention. After pizza, M&Ms, and yet another icebreaker game, the RA introduced our charge of creating a joint compact and handed out cards and pens, asking each person to write down something in the way of a rule or a "don't" that she would like to obtain for the hall. When we'd finished, the RA taped an enormous blank sheet of white paper to the wall, stood next to it with a marker, and said, "Tell me some of your items." Reluctantly and slowly, each person volunteered some rule. "Don't be too loud at night"; "Close the shower curtain so it doesn't flood the little anteroom"; "Don't leave your hair in the drain"; "Keep your door open when you're in your room (unless you're studying/sleeping)"; "Wipe your hair off of the shower walls"; "Don't take showers too long if there are people waiting."

There was no real discussion of any of the items. After everyone contributed, the RA took the sheet off the wall and left us to our candy. About one week later a large printed poster appeared on the hall, titled "Community Living Agreement," listing eight items, half of them pertaining to showers and a few to hair.

The same process occurred during the second semester, although shower etiquette had a lower priority. Six items were posted in the hall for our second semester community agreement:

Keep hair off the shower walls.
Keep doors open while you're chillin'.
Sleepovers and parties on the hall are cool.
Yell "flushing" if there's someone in the shower [because the shower water turned scalding during the flush].
No writing on the bathroom stall walls [this was the RA's].
Say "hi" to people to be friendly.

Although the agreement no doubt reflected some important values held by the residents, including sociability, courtesy, and cleanliness, it was the relationship of the individuals to the community agreement that interested me most. There had been no road map for actually creating an agreement, no mechanism for turning individual opinions into a community document. No one, including the RA, was comfortable suggesting that we might modify, prioritize, or remove individuals' suggestions from the list. While the seven students in attendance were considered to "represent" the others, because the latter did not show up to participate, there was no means for making the "agreement" binding on hall residents. As a result, the list remained posted for a semester, but each student on the hall decided whether she would abide by the agreement or not.

I never once heard anyone yell "flushing" in the bathroom, nor did I ever see a "cool sleepover" or public party on the hall. It seemed to me that the same people who kept their doors open prior to the agreement, including me, were the ones who kept their doors open afterward. There was never any follow-up or discussion about whether our agreement was being honored.

Community in the American university is paradoxically a private and an individual decision. As Robert Putnam documents in his history of community in the United States, *Bowling Alone,* the private decision to participate in community life is one that individuals in recent U.S. history are making less and less. From civic and religious life to political participation and informal social connections, there is an increasing individualism in American life that is evident in our universities as well.[6]

In such a historical light, the trends in dormitory living are thought-provoking. The newest dormitories being built across the country are both higher in amenities and lower in density than those of the past. It is no longer considered a viable model of campus life to have a hall full of people sharing a communal bathroom, lounge, and washing machine. The old blueprint of collective living has given way to much more individualized and opulent arrangements. Put in student lingo, individualism "rules."

At AnyU, new dorms are all built "suite-style," with four students sharing a huge apartment with four bedrooms and two bathrooms, as well as its own living room, kitchen, and washer-dryer units. The private bedrooms and semi-private bathrooms are more acceptable to contemporary students, who are no longer accustomed in childhood to sharing a room with a sibling. In fact, according to AnyU's Office of Residence Life, the number one reason why students move out of traditional dormitories is that they do not like sharing a communal bathroom. Dormitories, like campus life as a whole, are increasingly privatized, well appointed, and focused on an ever smaller network of people that constitutes the significant living community of the student.

These national trends bring into clearer focus the use of space in my own dormitory, a building constructed in the 1940s for a 1940s student. One can see how new students with new values have refashioned the existing space. The dormitory includes big, cushy public spaces filled with overstuffed furniture which appear to be expecting a crowd. There are lounges on each floor, one with a fireplace and some with large outside terraces; they have tables and chairs, community TVs and VCRs.

After using these spaces as a student, I began to realize something that I subsequently checked by monitoring more public lounges in my dorm and others: fellow students didn't really use these areas as social space. With the exception of the cleaning staff on their lunch breaks, I never saw students bring food and eat together, sit and socialize together, or even watch television together in our local lounge. During the course of an entire semester, what could be called "community life" or even "social activity" was extremely sparse. I saw one or two card games in the lounge on my floor, one simulation game meeting, scattered study groups that assembled in the dorm to work on a class project, and a Christian group who occasionally used the space to work on volunteer projects.

My observations of lounges in other dormitories were not significantly different. These spaces often sat empty. During the day, no one used them at all. On most nights, the overstuffed couches and chairs in our largest lounge would be draped with one to three students who had positioned themselves as far as possible from one another. Interviews with the few students who *were* in the lounges during my observations revealed that the majority came there to "get away"—from a gathering in their room, music blasting on the hall, or a roommate with a guest. In other words, the community spaces were often a *retreat* from social interaction, a way to create more private options. They were no longer, as their builders had probably envisioned, primarily a place for people to come together and participate in joint activities.

One of my greatest epiphanies about community life in the dorm came on Super Bowl Sunday. I had sneaked home Saturday night, intending to stay at my own house until Sunday night, when I realized that on Sunday afternoon at 2 PM Super Bowl coverage would begin, and I needed to be at the dorm. The event had been advertised heavily in the hall for weeks. "Free Ticket," the flyers read, and the "ticket" entitled one to good company, free pizza, and drinks during the game. The large lobby had been set up with two big-screen TVs so as to accommodate viewers from any vantage point.

I arrived a little early to get a good seat and waited for the lobby lounge to fill, but by game time there were only five other people in the space. One had tuned the second TV set to a different program, so I and four others watched the opening kickoff together. A couple of months earlier, when I had been the only one in the lounge for the World Series, I simply assumed that the event was under-advertised and that this generation had no love of baseball. When I saw that the same no-show pattern had occurred with the well-publicized football event, I decided to investigate further. Where were the other students? I left at halftime.

Many, I surmised, had gone to sports bars. But as I wandered the floors of my dorm, I could hear the game playing from numerous rooms. On my corridor alone, where there were two open doors, I could see clusters of people in each room eating and drinking as they watched the game together on their own sizable television sets. It seemed telling to me that so many dormitory residents were watching the same game in different places, the great majority preferring to pass the time with a carefully chosen group of personal friends in their own private space. It spoke in a more general way to how community really worked in the university.

Rather than being located in its shared symbols, meetings, activities, and rituals, the university for an undergraduate was more accurately a world of self-selected people and events. The university community was experienced by most students as a relatively small, personal network of people who did things together. This "individual community" was bolstered by a university system that honors student choice, as well as a level of materialism in the larger society that, by enabling students to own their own cars, computers, TV sets, and VCRs, renders collective resources and spaces superfluous. These characteristics of American university life—individualism, choice, and materialism—stand out even more clearly in chapter 4, where foreign students at AnyU describe and compare their own educational systems.

AnyU's Real Community: The Ego-Centered Network

When I asked students in interviews whether they felt they had a "community" at AnyU, most said yes. But what they meant by community were these personal networks of friends that some referred to as my "homeys." It was these small, ego-centered groups that were the backbone of most students' social experience in the university.

On a daily basis these personal networks were easily recognizable within the dorm and on campus. "Where are you now?" says the cell phone caller walking back to the dorm from class. "I'm on my way home, so ask Jeffrey and Mark to come, and I'll meet you at my room at 8." Such conversations are everywhere. In the dorm, residents can be heard discussing the timing and location of dinners and after-dinner plans, and message boards record the social negotiations: "Be home by 5:30. What about Mexican? Call me—P." Creating one's community involved very conscious choices to make one's leisure hours jibe with selected others'. There were few open invitations in these exchanges. Unless the RA had planned an activity, there was no general call to join in on dinner plans or come watch a video in someone's room.

Among members of the same network, however, there were constant interactions, ranging from borrowing detergent and snacks, to arranging social and shopping trips, to watching TV or videos together, to working out. The communications among network members occurred both publicly, like the planning just noted, and privately, as I saw in student diaries, where frequent cell phone contact and Instant Messaging sessions were the norm.

The intense reciprocity of ego-based groups helped explain a problem about campus traffic that had long puzzled me. As a professor, I could never understand why campus roads were so hopelessly jammed between classes. After all, AnyU had a campus bus system, and students had parking permits only for the lots adjacent to their dorms. They couldn't legally park at classroom building lots and would receive a hefty ticket if they did.

When I pasted my student parking pass on my car, I found myself basically grounded—able to drive off campus and back to my dorm but nowhere else. Why, then, were the roads so crowded with cars seemingly traveling from dorms to classes?

It wasn't long before I saw message boards with reminders such as "Tara, don't forget to pick me up 10 AM at the Social Science building.—L." Or "Be out in the Education Parking Lot at 3:10—Nick." As I walked or took the bus to class, I began to pay more attention to the non-dormitory parking lots and realized that there was a vast web of personal relationships activated for dropping and picking up passengers. It was network reciprocity at work.

These personal networks grew in importance to me as I realized their salience in the life of my fellow students, and in the life of the university. I became increasingly interested in how friends are made, how groups are formed, and how activities are coordinated. I built these queries in to my interviews and discovered much that observation alone did not tell me.

Student networks, like family relations, are ego based. In a family, even your first cousin will have relatives that you don't have in common, and the same is true of two students who are in each other's networks. Pam and Terry are part of the same social network, but when they separately name their own closest friends, the names are not exactly the same. Pam includes her boyfriend and his roommate along with Alice and Marie in her close network, while Terry includes Alice, Marie, and Pam but also a friend from class whom Pam barely knows. And Pam's boyfriend shares only a few of Pam's friends. One student's network, although it may overlap with those of others, is essentially personal; no two people share the exact same group of friends. This is what is meant by ego based: even these intimate forms of community are quite individual.

Most students, I found, had established a network of two to six friends who formed their core university community. From the "native" point of view, they got together because "we like each other." Students regularly named personality traits and

attitudes to explain their attraction to friends: "They're outspo-
ken"; "We're all a little weird"; "We like to have fun"; They're
"strong-minded and focused like me"; they're "up for anything, and pretty laid back"; "We're the same when it comes to
school, not big party-ers"; or they're "real friendly, open, responsible people."

To an outsider, especially an outsider who is looking at the
points of convergence among a number of students, student
networks have less to do with personality than with shared circumstances and shared demographics. Kyle, a Christian student on the floor, had a network of close friends for whom
being Christian was very important. They'd met while they
were still in high school, after attending several retreats that
happened to be held at AnyU. By the time they came to AnyU
as freshmen, they were already friends. The close networks of
five of the six minority students in my sample contained several other minority students. A number of them had met their
closest friends in an intensive pre-college summer program for
first-generation students, where there had been a sizable percentage of minority students. One of the most surprising findings to me was the discovery that eight of fourteen students interviewed about the subject of social networks had one or more
people in their close personal networks whom they knew from
high school or their hometown. In all, then, many of the networks that endured through college were based on experiences
before college, and these were conditioned by demographic
characteristics such as religion, race, ethnicity, and/or hometown (itself a function of race, ethnicity, religion, and class).

Once in school, it was also edifying to learn how early the
enduring friendships occurred in students' college life, and
how little they drew on academic interests and contacts. Most
students whose friends were cultivated after college began had
met their closest friends by virtue of living in the same freshman dorm or floor. Classroom contacts figured relatively little
in the social networks of students; fewer than one-quarter of
my interview students had met a member of their network in

an academic class or in an activity or club related to their major, while almost as many had met a close friend through ROTC or work.

Despite the belief that college expands our social horizons and extends our experience to include new and different types of people, the findings suggest otherwise. The most significant relationships are formed either before college or very early in one's college career, most often in some shared affiliation, whether voluntary or not, such as freshman dorm assignment, special freshman summer program, ROTC, ethnic club, or sorority and fraternity rush.

Diaries and interviews confirmed that for many students, their social lives at the university consisted of repeated contacts with the same people, who constituted that student's personal network. Once networks were formed, usually by the end of the freshman year, students tended to stay with their groups, maintaining intense and frequent interactions with their network and more superficial and sparse contacts with others. The way that student social life is formed necessarily affects issues of diversity.

Diversity at AnyU?

Student networks may be able to explain, at least in part, the failed diversity efforts at many universities, and certainly at AnyU. About 22 to 25 percent of AnyU students are considered "minority" by federal standards, and minority students appear approximately in these percentages in AnyU dorms and classes. What makes diversity a "success" in a state university, however, is not only that the university population reflects the diversity of the general population but also that students become more involved in the lives and issues of that diverse population. Part of that diversity ideal is the hope that all students will develop friends and have important conversations with those of backgrounds and ethnicities different from their own.

The National Survey of Student Engagement tries to capture

this information by asking a student to self-report as to whether he or she has "had serious conversations with students of a different race or ethnicity than your own." In 2003, fifty percent of college seniors nationwide indicated that they "often" or "very often" had such conversations, while only 13 percent said they did not.

This jibed with the information I initially was getting from my interviews about social networks, where I was finding that many students named someone from a different ethnic group within their close circle of friends. The interview information, though, did not match my direct observations, and this led me to probe further by fiddling with my interview questions and format. I soon realized that if I started, as I had, by asking informants whether they had close friends from other ethnic groups, the majority of students would say that they did. If I questioned them further, they would name that man from a class, or woman on the same intramural volleyball team, with whom they had close contact and describe how they met.

If, however, I started by asking informants to name their closest friends and then later asked them to identify the ethnicity of the named people, it turned out that most students, but white students predominantly, ended up becoming close friends with people of their own ethnicity. Since I thought that this "names first, ethnicity later" approach was more accurate, I changed the order of my questions and arrived at a very different picture. Five out of six white students I interviewed in this way about their networks had no members of another racial or ethnic group in their close social circle; the networks of five of the six minority students contained one or more minorities (more on the details of this later).

One can see from the descriptions of how networks form why this might be true. Many students are building on contacts developed before they entered college, contacts that have strong demographic and social components. If many student networks begin with hometown contacts, what is the likelihood that they will cross class, ethnic, race, or even religious lines when the United States is demographically divided along precisely these lines? Although there was one instance in my data of a cross-racial network pair with its origin in high school, the probabilities in this country work strongly the other way because of de facto neighborhood and school segregation. All other examples I found of high school or hometown friends in an AnyU network involved a woman or man of the same ethnicity as the person interviewed.

Even many relationships developed early in college contain a built-in bias. Although classes and interest clubs may be ethnically well mixed, this is not where students make their earliest school contacts. Freshman dorms are generally well integrated, but not several of the early programs and events that help introduce and acclimate new students, including Previews weekends designated for particular ethnic groups, pre-college "outdoor adventure" trips that cost extra money, a summer program for first-generation college students, or the opening round of sorority and fraternity mixers. Some institutional structures like these may encourage the early formation of same-ethnicity relationships.

There is no doubt that active racism also plays a part in the lack of diversity on college campuses. Yet, race or ethnicity is typically ignored as a topic of conversation in mainstream college culture, treated as an invisible issue and with silence. As Levine and Cureton (1998) found in their nationwide survey, students were "more willing to tell intimate details of their sex lives than discuss race relations on campus."[7] When the subject *is* raised, as in the occasional class, students of color report being continually expected to educate whites about minority issues or speak "as a representative of their race."

Despite the general invisibility of the subject of race in informal student culture, there was not a single minority student I interviewed who hadn't experienced racism.[8] Few openly complained, but everyone had at least one story to tell of comments made in class, rude remarks on the street, or just hostile looks. When I asked Pat, a Hispanic–Native American woman, whether she had ever considered rushing a sorority, she told me that she had in her freshman year, but "I could see that it wasn't really right for me, because I'd pass by all the sorority tables—you know how they call out to girls to come over and take a look—well, I saw they called out to other girls but not to me. They just kinda ignored me, not hostile or anything, but not interested either."

"It's just how it is," another female student explained. "There are some good people and some not so good people, and you deal with it."

Who Eats with Whom: A Study of Student Dining

My very small sample of student networks and interviews was suggestive to me but not convincing that diversity in student relationships was in serious question. So I decided to conduct a larger observational study of students' informal social behavior. I chose eating as the focus, one of my favorite social activities, and asked the research question "Who eats with whom?" This seemed a fair and appropriate inquiry into diversity, to determine the range of people with whom one breaks bread.

It was my most extensive and longest-running "mini-study" of campus life. For five months I directly observed and recorded the dining behavior of fellow students during randomly selected periods of the day at optional dining areas on campus.[9] Although some patrons carried out their food, returning to their dorms or outside benches to eat, many ate and drank singly or in groups at the various tables provided in one of five eating areas I surveyed. Sitting at a different table in the room, I would record who sat at each table by gender and, as much as outward appearances can signal, ethnicity.

It is always problematic to do research like this, because there is a wide range of appearances for all ethnicities, and many sticky issues. My interest, however, *was* in appearances, and in seeing to what extent students chose to share food and conversation with people who looked like them (or, more accurately, seemed to belong in the same broad ethnic category that an observer would attribute to them). Although there are other kinds of diversity (e.g., age), I recorded only the data reflecting each person's gender and, to the extent possible, his or her category of ethnicity such as white non-Hispanic, Hispanic, Asian, African American, Native American, and so on. These were not easy calls. Sometimes I could tell only that someone was not a white non-Hispanic but couldn't identify the more specific group to which she or he belonged; at other times I could not tell whether a person was white and non-Hispanic or something else.

In gathering this information I had these questions in mind: To what extent did informal university activities (e.g., eating together) convey diversity? Did students eat in same or mixed ethnic and gender groups? Were there differences in the eating patterns of dominant (defined as white non-Hispanic) and non-dominant (defined as people of color) ethnic groups? Did any ethnic group or category eat alone more often than others?

I analyzed the data with regard to these questions but took care to analyze by person rather than by table in order to try to see the data through the eyes of the particular diner. For instance, if there were a table consisting of four people—a white male, two white women, and one Hispanic woman—each would have a different reality at the table: the male is eating with a table of all women of mixed ethnicity; both white women are eating at a table of mixed gender and mixed ethnicity; and the Hispanic woman is eating at a mixed-gender table where everyone is of a different ethnicity from herself. I recorded the data, preserving the perspective of each diner, and then analyzed the data in ten different categories that allowed me to examine the relationship of each table diner to the rest.[10] In this way, I tracked almost 1,500 examples of dining behavior.

What I found was interesting. It showed not only an overall lack of diversity, as national studies report,[11] but also the existence of huge differences in the diversity experiences of dominant and non-dominant groups. Minorities (people of color) ate alone only slightly more often: one-quarter of minority women and more than one-third of minority men sitting in public spaces ate alone, a rate greater than that for white women and men by 3 percent and 5 percent, respectively. But of all those who ate with others, only 10 percent of white men and 14 percent of white women ate at a table where there was anyone of a different color from themselves. Only 2.6 percent and 3.5 percent of white men and women, respectively, ate at a table of two or more where they were the only white person. The statistics were strikingly different for people of color: 68 percent of women and 58 percent of men ate with "mixed groups." People of color were ten times more likely than whites to eat in a group in which they were the only person of a different race/ethnicity at the table.

The same patterns I saw in the dining spaces proved true in the composition of personal networks when I compared a group of twelve students on my hall, six whites and six students of color. Although the networks of Caucasian students included more whites, and those of people of color more minorities, the total networks of minority students were primarily "mixed," comprising people of various ethnicities, including whites. One student of color was in an all-white network, while another had friends of only her own ethnicity. By contrast, five of the six white students had networks that were solidly white; only one white student had a mixed network, and none was the only Caucasian.

Seen in this context, minority ethnic clubs, dorms, and student unions have a clearer meaning. Ethnic-based groups are often clouded by perceptions that they, like the Greek system, remove their members from the mainstream and surround them with people of the same background. What the data suggest to me is that people of color are already heavily involved in interethnic and interracial relationships on campus. In fact, most of their informal dining contacts, as well as personal networks, included people who were ethnically different from them. Under these circumstances, an ethnic-based club—which half of the minorities in my sample thought was important in their lives—is better understood as a needed respite from difference, a chance to rest comfortably with others who share similar experiences in the world.

It was white students, most markedly males, whose social lives suffered from a lack of diversity. When white men *did* eat with those of different ethnicities, the majority of tables were "cross-gender." In other words, white men socialized at meals to a greater degree with nonwhite women or with groups that included nonwhite women. There was extremely little contact between white and nonwhite men. Only 4 of 489 white males, fewer than 1 percent, ate with (only) males of a different ethnicity, but 31 ate in different or mixed ethnic groups in which women were present. Men of color, while much more diverse in their dining, followed a similar pattern, tending to have fewer cross-ethnic male-only eating partners (7 of 79) while favoring cross-ethnic tables where women were eating too (24 of 79). The same pattern was not true of women. For both white women and women of color, their cross-color contact was primarily with other women.

One of the more disturbing but confusing findings was how few people of color, proportionally, used the common eating spaces. Only 13 percent of the entire dining sample was nonwhite, while 22 percent of full-time students were nonwhite. This left more than 40 percent of the minority population unaccounted for. There are certainly many ways to interpret what was going on. Perhaps this eyeballing approach to minority status simply fails to recognize many who are legal minorities. Perhaps there are economic factors at work that bear on having a meal ticket or buying food during the day that disadvantage some minority students. Perhaps the difference is explained by the larger percentage of minority students who enroll in off-campus programs. But there is another possibility that I entertained, which was related to my finding that more minority students eat alone.

My evidence is only anecdotal because I didn't formally monitor what I thought I was seeing, but this is what I noticed. I would observe the food court area as people got their food and stood in line to pay, watching each person leave the register to see where he or she went to sit in order to mark it in my book. I often found that instead of going to a table, however, a person of color would go to a condiment area, pack up a napkin and the food in a bag, and leave. It seemed to me that a greater proportion of minorities was leaving.

One day, as I was just finishing an observation session, an African American woman left the register and headed for a table. She would be the last diner to enter my monitored space in the set time period. I prepared to mark her table choice, but instead of sitting down, she readjusted her backpack, took her food, and left. Where is she going? I asked myself. To meet a friend in a different area? To eat outside? I felt a bit like a stalker as I followed her out of the dining area and out of the building. She passed the outdoor tables and kept walking until she entered one of the freshman dorms, went through the lobby, and up the stairs. My guess was that she had returned to eat in her dorm room.

I will never know for sure what lay behind that one observation, or what I perceived to be the larger proportion of students of color who did not stay to eat. But it left me with the uncomfortable feeling that I was witnessing the effect of a "white space"—which I had never noticed because I am white—where people of color could eat alone publicly, or eat with people different from themselves, or go home to their rooms. Perhaps, many times, the dorm room just seems the most comfortable option, and this may have explained some of the missing 40 percent of minority students in the dining areas.

The ideals of community and diversity are certainly in place at AnyU and remain important components of stated university policy. Yet neither is fully realized in university culture, as I believe I have illustrated in this chapter. What I also hope I've illustrated, though, is what anthropologists mean when they say that a culture cannot really be divided into its parts; one part of a culture cannot be understood in isolation from its other parts, and all must be contextualized within the larger whole. Culture, we argue, is both integrated and holistic.

In just this way "community" and "diversity" are parts of university culture, but they are not intelligible on their own. As the descriptions of student life attest, diversity is one part of college culture that is intimately tied to community, another part. And both parts are ultimately conditioned by structures in the larger American society—including values of individualism and choice, materialism, and the realities of U.S. demographics—that may seem, at first, to have little bearing on whether college diversity increases because freshmen Joe and Juan truly become friends, or whether Jane strengthens community by deciding to attend Movie Night. But they do. Not understanding this leads to a reality about diversity and community in university culture that does not match its rhetoric, and a persistent confusion about why this is so.

CHAPTER 4

As Others See Us

As a partial outsider in college owing to my age, I found myself drawn to other partial outsiders, and vice versa. Those of us who in some way deviated from the norm perceived something in common and ended up, I noted, seeking one another out. Thus, the transfer student on my hall became a friend; I was close, too, to the more withdrawn and rural students at Previews, the lone African American student in my freshman seminar, and the international students in my dorms and classes.

My conversations with students from other countries were often illuminating. As anthropologists have come to know, culture can be invisible to its natives—so taken for granted that it seems unworthy of comment. Although I could view student life with an outsider-professor's eye, there was much about the U.S. college scene that, in its familiarity, was invisible to me as well. The more I spoke with international students, the more I noticed familiar refrains that both educated me and reminded me about my own U.S. and academic culture. After having many such informal conversations with both international students and teachers, I decided to add formal interviews of international students to my investigation of U.S. college life. In all, I conducted thirteen formal interviews, as well as several informal conversations, which included perspectives from Somalia,

England, Japan, Germany, China, Mexico, Spain, the United Arab Emirates, India, Malaysia, France, and Korea. In this chapter I share the comments made and stories told by international students as they grappled to understand and to fit in at AnyU.[1] Their struggles, surprises, and dilemmas pointed to both mundane and profound revelations about U.S. students, professors, and the college education system.

Getting to Know "American" Students

One of my earliest international contacts was with a young Japanese woman, Toshi, who lived on my floor. During Welcome Week, after we played volleyball together, I introduced myself and began a casual conversation. When I saw her again at a workshop, we eyed each other like long-lost friends, and she introduced me to two Japanese friends accompanying her who lived in other dorms. The four of us talked enjoyably for a while, and it was clear that the three exchange students were pleased to be engaged by an American student in this first week of activities.[2] I told them that I'd like to make dinner for them, and departed intending to stop by Toshi's room and ask her to invite her two friends to a Friday night dinner at our dorm. As I left, though, one of the women (whom I'll call Chiho) asked me a brave question in slightly halting English: "Excuse me but I don't understand. How can we have dinner together if you don't have my phone number and I don't have yours?"

I saw her confusion. After exchanging telephone numbers with all three women for assurance, I asked Chiho whether people had invited her before without following up. "I think so," she responded "but I'm not sure. I have been here for two months and I am still very confused by the customs. American students are so friendly and so nice. They are so open about wanting to get together, but they never take my phone number and they never contact me again. When I see a woman I met two days ago, she does not seem to know me or remember my name."

I winced at the truth of the friendly American veneer. "Nice to meet you," "Drop by," "See you soon," all sounded like authentic invitations for further contact. And yet the words were without social substance. It was not just Japanese, or even non-Western, students for whom deciphering friendliness was a problem. One German student commented: "There are some surface things about American friendliness. Like 'How are you?' A girl asked me that one day when I was feeling sick, and I answered that I wasn't too good but she just went on like I had never said that. Maybe it's a sign of caring to say that. But in Germany, 'How are you?' is the actual start of a conversation rather than just a hi/good-bye."

Meeting and befriending Americans in more than a superficial way presented challenges to many international students. Even in class, students found it difficult. One Asian student told me how, in her linguistics class, the teacher had told the class that the native speakers should try to include international students in their groups for the study project. "But when we formed the groups," she recounted, "nobody even responded or asked us to be in their groups, so the international students had to make their own group."

In some ways, their dilemma was like my own. Where is community in the American university, and how does one become a part of it? International students learned quickly that being a student, being a dorm mate, being a classmate—none of it automatically qualifies you as a "member of the community," that is, someone whom others will seek out for activities.

"In Korea," one woman told me, "if we all take class together and our class ends at lunchtime, we would go out together as a group." No such group outing was available as a way for new students to meet others in their classes. Because in Japan, creating a network of friends and contacts is a major purpose of going to college, Midori found it surprising that U.S. students "leave the classroom right after class is over. They come to class to get a grade, not to meet people or talk to people. They leave right away and don't talk to other people. I don't get why students run out of class, packing up and running out immediately."

Many students expressed surprise at the dull reception they received and the lack of interest they perceived from American students about their experiences and backgrounds. "Students don't ask me anything about my life," a Somali student lamented. "Even my friends . . . they don't ask me questions about how I got here, or my life in other places." A student from the United Arab Emirates observed: "Here everyone minds their own business. They're not that hospitable. Like if someone from the U.S. came to the UAE, people would take them out to eat and ask questions. It would be a long time before they paid for their own meal." A Mexican student concurred: "I'm lonely here. I don't think an American coming to Mexico would have the same experience as I've had here. We're more social, more curious. We'd be talking to him and asking questions."

"When I talk to them," one Japanese woman noted with dismay about her American classmates, "they don't try to understand what I say or keep up the conversation. They don't keep talking, and I realize that they don't want to take the trouble to talk with me." She thought that maybe the problem had to do with her thick accent. When I asked another Japanese student what questions students had asked him about his country, he answered: "Well, mostly nobody asks me anything about Japan. Some Americans don't care about other worlds. They don't ask questions, but those that do sometimes know more about Japan than I do."

Almost all international students discovered some individuals who were interested in their lives, but it was much more the exception than the rule, and these tended to be U.S. students who were well traveled or who had been exchange students themselves. "What I miss most," admitted one student, "is to have someone to talk to, to feel that someone else is interested in you." A Mexican student agreed: "I've met people who are interested in me, but for a lot of other people it's . . . 'whatever'! My [car] mechanic is more interested in my life and my background than other students."

It was difficult, even for someone born in the United States, to see that the outward openness of both college and American life was often coupled with a closed attachment to a small set of relationships, many of them (as we saw in chapter 2) developed early in college and focused on people of very similar background. International students were often forced into the same structure, finding that despite their interest in forming friendships with Americans, they seemed to end up in relationships with other "foreigners." In many ways the active international programs, which ran socials and trips for its students, reinforced a pattern in which international students came in contact mostly with other non–U.S.-born students.

It was interesting to me that, echoing the camaraderie I felt with "others," a number of international students indicated that they found it easier to get to know U.S. minority students than white students. One student told me, "They [minorities] seem to be less gregarious than other Americans, in the sense that they seem not to have as many friends and they are looking [shyly] for people themselves." In practice, despite the fact that many students had come to the United States expressly for the "international experience," the majority fraternized with other foreign students.

"I think I know how to meet Americans," Beniko, a Japanese student, told me, "because my boyfriend meets people and has some American friends. It's his interests." Beniko explained to me that Americans find relationships when they identify hobbies or elective interests in common. She went on: "My boyfriend likes playing the drums, and he plays them in the dorms and people come into his room. They're like a friend magnet. It's the same with martial arts. He likes that, and other boys do too, and they watch videos together, like Jackie Chan. If you don't have a hobby in this country, it's harder to meet people. I need to develop a hobby."

Relationships and Friendships

Both Midori and Reiko had been excited, if a little nervous, to be assigned an American roommate. It was surprising to Reiko that there was no formal introduction; roommates met, instead, when they both happened to be in the room at the same time. Midori had heard that many Americans were messy and loud, but she knew that wasn't true across the board and hoped her roommate would not fit the stereotype.

As it turned out, Midori's roommate—neat and fairly quiet—*was* different from her expectations, but she presented challenges on another level. She spent most days and nights at her boyfriend's apartment, returning only one or two days a week to their room. And when she did, as Midori explained, her personal and spatial boundaries were sharp:

> It bothers her if I change anything in the room, even though she only came to the room one or two times a week. She would say, "This is my window—don't open it"—even if she is not there and I am very hot! "Don't change the heater setting." I ask her, "Can I turn on the light now?" "Can I put some food in your refrigerator?" It had almost nothing in it. After a while, she just comes back to the room and ignores me. She let me know that I am her roommate and nothing more.

The separateness and individualism of the roommate relationship was something that Reiko encountered as well, albeit without the hostility. Her roommate had also communicated that they would be "roommates and nothing more," but Reiko came to appreciate the advantages of this arrangement:

> I like the American system. My roommate is just my roommate. In [my country] I would be worrying and thinking all the time about my roommate. If I want to go to dinner, I feel I have to ask my roommate, "Have you eaten yet?

Would you like to go to dinner?" I must ask her about her classes and help her if she has a problem. Here I have a roommate and I work separately. I don't have to care about her. It's easier.

International students saw "individualism" and "independence" as characteristic not only of roommate interactions but of relations with family and friends as well. When Arturo was asked about how AnyU students differed from those in his own country, he responded: "There's much more independence here. At home, students live with their parents. Here families aren't that tied together. My roommates call their dads and moms maybe once a week, and that's it. It would be different if they were Mexican." Alicia, another Mexican student, thought similarly that "Americans have a lot of independence. At eighteen in Mexico, I can't think of living by myself. Maybe it's the money, but we think united is better, for both family ties and for expenses."

For Peter from Germany, Nadif from Somalia, and Nigel from England, the disconnection from family had repercussions for social life with friends. Americans, they felt, sharply distinguished their family from their friends and schoolmates; more than one international student remarked about the dearth of family photos on student doors, as if family didn't exist at school. International students generally saw family as more naturally integrated into their social lives. "When you're not near your family," Peter told me, "it's hard to know where do I invite people. No one here says, 'Come on and meet my family.' Here I have to invite people to come to a home with two other people I don't know. It's strange."

Nadif continued in a similar vein:

I have American friends, but I haven't been to their houses. I don't know their parents or their brothers and sisters or families. Back home, if I have a friend, everyone in their family knows me and I know them. If I go over to visit [friends] and they're not there, I still stay and talk with their family. Here friendship doesn't involve families. I don't know where my friends live and who their families are.

Nigel found the American system peculiar, much less similar to his own culture than he had expected. "My friends come to my house, and they just walk in. It's like they're friends not just with me but with my family. You know, a lot of my friends' parents buy me Christmas presents." He went on:

If I have a party—like at Christmas I had a big party—my mum and dad, they'd just join in and drink with everyone else and have a good time. My American friends would think that's daft. I have friends [at AnyU] who have all grown up in the same city near one another. They wouldn't know how to have a conversation with anyone else's parents. They get their friends to come over when their parents are out, like, "Hey, my parents are away, come on over." At home, it doesn't make a difference whether your parents are there or not.

For Alicia from Mexico, this was all evidence of American "independence." But "independence," she argued, was one side of a coin. The other side "is that I'm not sure that they have real friendships."

The issue of real friendship was often more problematic in interviews than I had anticipated. I typically asked what I considered to be a straightforward question: "Do you have friends who are American?"

"I'm not sure," answered one Japanese girl. "My American roommate might be a friend."

"What makes you unsure?" I queried further.

"Well, I like my roommate," she explained, "and sometimes even I cook and we eat together at home, but since August [six months earlier] we have gone out together three times. That's really not much, not what friends would do in my country, so I don't know."

Another student responded to my question about friends with one of his own. "What do you mean by 'friend,'" he asked, "*my* version or the American version?" A French student responded quickly to my query about friends: "Sure I have friends. It's so easy to meet people here, to make friends." Then she added: "Well, not really friends. That's the thing. Friendship is very surface-defined here. It is easy to get to know people, but the friendship is superficial. We wouldn't even call it a friendship. In France, when you're someone's friend, you're their friend for life." Their trouble answering my question taught me something: There were recurring questions about what constitutes friendship for Americans.

A prime difficulty in sorting out the concept centered on judgments surrounding what one did for a friend. When Maria made her first American "friends," she expected that they would be more active in helping her settle in her new home.

> I was living in a new country and I needed help. Like with setting up a bank account and doing the lease. It was new for me. And looking for a mechanic to fix my car. Or going shopping—I didn't know what to buy [for my room]. And when I tell my friends that I had a hard day trying to figure out all the things they say, "Oh, I'm so sorry for you."

Maria found it unfathomable. "In Mexico, when someone is a friend, then regardless of the situation, even if I would get in trouble, I would help them. American people are always busy. 'Oh, I like you so much,' they say. But then if I'm in trouble, it's, 'Oh, I'm so sorry for you.' 'So sorry for you' doesn't help!"

Geeta's roommates seemed just the opposite. When she told them that she was planning on buying a used car, they told her, "Oh, you don't need a car. We have two cars and one of us will take you where you want to go." But then after a while, she explained,

> I see how life is here. It's like I'm a little eight-year-old girl, and I have to say. "Could someone please take me here?"

"Could someone take me there?" So I don't ask much. One day I said that I need a ride to school, and my roommate says, "Fine, but you have to leave right now," and now isn't when I want to go. After a while, I saw that I needed my own car.

Nigel told me: "I don't understand the superficiality in friendships here. Americans are much friendlier than the English, but then it doesn't really go anywhere. As far as deep friendships are concerned—I know there are people who have deep friendships, but it's a lot harder to figure out who those people will be." I asked him, "What's so different about friendship at home?"

I think friends at home are closer. We're in touch every day, for one thing. For another, when one person is doing something, the others are supporting them. Here one of my American friends graduated, and I went to the graduation to support him. A lot of our other friends were here for graduation, but they didn't even go to watch him graduate, and they weren't even doing anything. That upset me. There's a lot of incidents like that. It's confusing.

"Confusing," "funny," "peculiar" were all words used to describe American social behavior. "Why do so many students eat alone in their rooms rather than go out or cook together?" "Why don't any of the guys on my hall know how to cook anything?" "Why does everyone here use computers [Instant Messaging] to communicate with people who are down the hall or in the same dorm?" "Why do young Americans talk so much about *relationships*?"

The *way* that Americans socialized was also a prime subject of comment. Two points stood out. First, Americans don't socialize as much, tending to spend more time alone, as this British student explained:

People back home of my age socialize a lot more. On a free night, you'd go out and meet friends and be doing something together. You'd probably go out as a big group. In a week of seven days, I'd probably go out two or three nights. It's all student-based and promoted. Here, in the evenings, you walk down the hall and people are sitting in their rooms playing video games and watching television.

The second thing consistently noticed by international students is how Americans seem to separate socializing and partying from the rest of their lives. "Social life in Japan," explained one student, "is different. It's not like, 'This is party time.' It's more integrated with the rest of your day and your life." A French student noted this same pattern, but with regard to clothing. "We'll be hanging out, and then we decide to go out. The American girl in the group says, 'I need to go home and change.' I think, why? It's the same people. We're just going to a different place now. We're not going to anyplace fancy. What is so different now that you have to go change your clothes?"

For one British student as well, the American "party time" mentality was perplexing:

I don't understand this party thing in the U.S. When you go out here, it's get drunk or nothing. If people go out with people and drink, they have to get drunk. If they don't get falling-down drunk, they think, "What's the point of doing it?" I find it difficult to understand. It's really a European thing. You socialize, have a few drinks together, and go home.

For many international students, then, there was more flow between family and friends, school and home, and between academics and social life.

Classroom Life

In the classroom, most foreign students notice what U.S. adults, if they have been away long from academia, would probably notice too: there is an informality to the U.S. college classroom that some, including professors, would interpret as bordering on disrespect. A Japanese student giggled as she told me: "It makes me laugh when I see how students come to class: shorts, flip-flops . . . torn T-shirts. Some students come to class in pajamas!" A Middle Eastern student exclaimed: "You have so much freedom here. You can step out of class in the middle of the class! We could never do that." For one Asian student, one of the surprises was how often students interrupt the professor in the middle of a lecture to ask their own questions. This would not be tolerated in his country. An African student shared his thoughts: "There are certain things that surprise me about American students. I look at how they drink and eat during class. They put their feet up on the chairs. They pack up their books at the end of class before the teacher has finished talking." One European student noted, "We used to eat and drink in class sometimes, but at least we hid it!"

Indeed, as any American college student knows, stepping out of class or interrupting a lecture with questions is now quite acceptable. Eating and drinking during class, sleeping openly, packing up books before the teacher has finished talking have come to be standard behavior that most professors will ignore.

For the most part, international students liked the American classroom and American professors. U.S. professors were described by different international students as "laid-back," "helpful," "open," "tolerant" (of scant clothing and sleeping in class), "casual," and "friendly." Some, like the UAE and Somali students, appreciated that "teachers are not as involved in your lives—they don't see where you live or try to force you to study." For others, including the Japanese and Korean students, it was the interest in listening to students' problems and opinions and in helping students that was refreshing:

> Teachers think helping students is their job. In Japan they don't think that way. I e-mailed my prof in Japan because I am doing an independent study and I asked her to send me an article. She got mad at me and thought this was very rude for me to ask her to do this.

American professors are more open; they give you their phone numbers and some let you call them at home. You can really talk to them outside of class and they are willing to give you extra help.

Although American professors and the American classroom received high marks for openness and helpfulness, they received mixed reviews on course content, including its rigor, organization, and modes of evaluation. Although one Indian student appreciated that "profs tell me which points to concentrate on when I read; they sometimes give chapter summaries so I know what to focus my attention on," more than one other mentioned the controlled way in which the American college classroom is run. The student is given a small chunk of reading and lecture to absorb, and then there is a test, usually short-answer format. Then there is another chunk of reading and a test. It is a system that one student described as "forced study," but one in which it's generally fairly easy to master the material and do well.

Most international students were used to a less pre-digested academic diet. Their course content was delivered by lecture, and it was students' responsibility to fully understand the content without the benefit of outlines, projected overhead notes, and other aids, as in the American classroom. Their grades for the semester would be based only on two long comprehensive essay exams and sometimes a lengthy theme paper. The American approach—frequent small short-answer tests sometimes coupled with study guides and lecture outlines—was criticized by different international students:

[It works but] in some ways . . . it's like elementary school or grade school. The teacher tells you exactly which chapters to study, and then you review just those chapters. The advisers tell you the courses to take and approve your schedule. Sometimes it's annoying.

Students here have lots of exams, really small quizzes. The quizzes make you study. You learn a little bit for the quiz, then you learn a little bit different for the next quiz. But people forget from week to week. Once the quiz is over, they forget. . . . Really, I wonder at the end of the semester what people remember when they leave.

I find it difficult to take the exams here seriously. You can go into a multiple-choice exam without studying really and still come out all right from things you remember from class, and a process of elimination. You could never go into an exam back home knowing nothing. They're essay, and you start from a blank page; you wouldn't know what to write. Knowing almost nothing there, you'd get a 20 percent. Here you could pass the test!

Still some students appreciated the American grading system, with smaller, non-comprehensive exams and a syllabus, serving almost as a contract that laid out exactly how tests, papers, and presentations would bear on the final grade. As one Asian student explained:

We don't know what we're getting for a grade in [my country]. We don't have small quizzes, just one final exam or sometimes two, and there's no class participation. I had a class that I thought I was doing well in but I got a C. Expectations are much clearer in the U.S. They are much clearer about grading. It's easier to see results of a test or paper and how it related to a grade in a course.

"Teaching in America is like a one-man show," argued Élène, a French student, in the middle of our interview. "Teachers tell jokes; they do PowerPoint. There is audience participation."

"I thought you just said that in France it was a one-man show," I followed up, "because the teacher basically just stood up with a microphone and lectured."

"Yeah, that's true" Élène went on, "but it's not entertainment. It's a lecture. They're not trying to interest and entertain the students, and where I went to school we never rated the professors, like entertainers, with evaluations at the end of every course."

Opinions of the U.S. system varied somewhat with a student's country of origin. While Mexican students found U.S. professors and advisers a little formal, most international students noted their easy informality. A Chinese student was alone in mentioning that "the profs don't seem to prepare as much. There is little in the way of class notes or handouts for the students." And while the UAE and Somali students believed that "U.S. students are more serious about school because it makes more of a difference to your future," for most international students, either the lack of rigor of American classes or the work attitudes of American students presented a different sort of surprise.

"When I was in Japan, I heard how hard it was to go to university in the U.S.," said one student, "but now I'm here and I see that many students don't do the work."

"How do you know that?" I asked.

She responded, "When I talk about an assignment, they say they didn't do it!" It's confusing, though, she admitted: "Students in my class complain a lot about the time commitment while, at the same time, they talk about the parties they go to and the drinking. Some students make the effort, but I see that many others don't do the work."

Most European students agreed that U.S. classes were less demanding. "My first two years of classes in this country," said Élène, "were at the high school level. What a joke! Only at the 300 and 400 level am I seeing much better and harder material." A British student commented: "My involvement within my actual classes is a lot higher here, but as far as the content of work, it's actually a lot easier. I didn't work nearly as hard as I could, and I got Bs and better in all of my classes." According to Li, Chinese students work harder and do more homework: "I don't think the American students work that hard. I did a group project with an American student and I see he follows. I organize. I suggest the books we should read because I want a good grade. He just comes to meetings but doesn't really prepare. At the end, he thanks me for carrying the project."

"Group work" was one of three points that were often repeated when I asked what if anything is different about the "academic approach" in the American classroom. I had never really thought about it until I saw how many international students noted the frequency of group projects and presentations in their classes. One European recounted: "Here they keep telling you to get into groups; do a presentation. I've done so many presentations while I've been here I can't believe it.... Many of them aren't even marked—we just do them as an exercise. I think it's a good thing, because people here get a lot more confident about talking in front of others."

"It's funny," I mused with Beniko, a Japanese student, "that in such an individual culture students do so much work in groups."

"I think I understand why you can," she answered. "It is because of your individualism. In Japan, we don't and couldn't do much group work because we would consider each other TOO MUCH, and the project would get very complicated because of that." Only American students, she suggested, would have the necessary boundaries and sense of their own preferences to be able to negotiate the demands of a group project.

Individualism and individual choice also figured into both of the other mentioned themes. For Asian students in particular, one formidable challenge of the American classroom was in the number of times people were asked to "say what they think." "Professors are always asking what you think of this and think of that," maintained one Japanese student. "It's great, but it's scary when you're not used to this. I don't always know what I think."

One Korean woman remarked to me:

Everything here is: "What do you want?" "What do you think?" "What do you like?" Even little children have preferences and interests in this country. I hear parents in restaurants. They ask a three-year-old child, "Do you want French fries or potato chips?" Every little kid in this country can tell you, "I like green beans but not spinach, I like vanilla but not chocolate, and my favorite color is blue." They're used to thinking that way.

"Choice" abounds in the U.S. educational system in ways that most American-born students are unaware of. "You can take [courses] that interest you here," affirmed one student. "If I like archaeology—good, I take it. But then I also like astronomy, so I take that." A Japanese student explained that at home she "can't take a ceramics course just because I like it." The courses she takes are determined by her major and not subject to choice. In Europe, another student told me, "when we get electives, we are able to choose from a very short list which course from the list you will take. You get very few 'open credits'—what *you* call electives—where you can actually pick the course, and it is usual for someone to take a course that is related to their major so it helps them with other courses."

In their home countries, most international students could not change their major, nor could they liberally choose classes outside their major, nor could they double-major or double-minor. Most could not drop courses after they were enrolled. For some international students, even being able to pick one's major was a luxury. In countries that rely heavily on test scores for entry into specific fields, one's major often depends on rankings on exams. A Japanese student reported: "Many people in Japan pick majors they don't want. My friend is studying to be an English teacher, but she wants to be a dog groomer. She picked her major based on her test results and what she did well in."

"There's a lot of choice in your curriculum," one Spanish student maintained, "and even in the time you take classes. In Spain, certain courses MUST be taken, and a class is given at one time and that's it."

The same choice inherent in the curriculum was seen in the extra-curriculum. "There are so many clubs to choose from here—you can pick any interest and there will be a club for it!" remarked an African student. "If you want to join a sport in my country," said another, "we have one or two sports you can join (soccer and cricket), but here you can choose from so many different ones like climbing, snowboarding, basketball, soccer, football—and so many more."

There were few detractors from the benefits of choice in the American system, but a couple of students pointed out the downside of having so *much* choice. One suggested: "Your system is much more complicated, and it's much less specialized. Because you take so many different kinds of courses, you are spread thinner and have less focused knowledge in particular areas." Another looked at the implications of students' freedom to drop a course at will: "People here can drop a class whenever they want. If I don't like it, I drop it. If I don't like the teacher, I drop it. If I'm not doing well, I drop it. In Spain, once you sign, you pay, and you can't drop. I think it affects attitude."

Indeed, as one foreign-born teacher confided, "I take time to talk to my students who didn't do well on an exam or who are having trouble. I suggest that they set up an appointment with me, and I tell them what skills they need to work on extra. The minute I do that, it has the opposite effect in your system. Instead of coming to my office, they drop the class. It's really quite surprising!"

Worldliness and Worldview

The single biggest complaint international students lodged about U.S. students was, to put it bluntly, our ignorance. As informants described it, by "ignorance" they meant the misinformation and lack of information that Americans have both about other countries and about themselves. Although most international students noted how little other students asked them about their countries, almost all students had received questions that they found startling: "Is Japan in China?" "Do you have a hole for a bathroom?" "Is it North Korea or South Korea that has a dictator?" "Where exactly is India?" "Do you still ride elephants?" "Do they dub American TV programs into British?"

These are just a few of the questions American students actually asked of international students. While they no doubt came from the less sophisticated among their classmates, it was clear that international students across the board felt that most Americans—even their own friends—are woefully ignorant of the world scene. It is instructive to hear how students from diverse countries discuss their perceptions of American students' views of themselves and the world.

JAPAN: Really, they don't know very much about other countries, but maybe it's just because a country like Japan is so far away. Japanese probably don't know about the Middle East. Sometimes, students keep asking about ninjas.

UAE: American students are nice, but they need to stop being so ignorant about other countries and other cultures. Americans need to look at the world around them, and even the cultures around them in their own country.

MEXICO: The U.S. is not the center of the world. [Americans] don't know anything about other countries. Many of them don't have an interest in learning about other cultures. The only things students ever ask me about in my culture is food.

CHINA: Americans know very little about China or its culture. Most people think China is still very poor and very communist-controlled, with no freedom. There is a very anticommunist feeling, and people know little about today's China, which is quite changing and different. New Zealanders know much more about China—perhaps it's their proximity. I think that older people here have more of a sense of history, and that history, about the wars, about the cold war, makes them understand more about the world. Younger people seem to have no sense of history.

ENGLAND: People here know surprisingly little about England, and they assume a lot of things, some true, some not. People's impressions of me when I say I'm from England is that I might drink tea off a silver tray, and maybe live in a castle, and use a red telephone box. That's the honest truth. The questions that I've been asked are unbelievable.

MALAYSIA: I tell people that I am Muslim, and they take for granted that I'm an Arab. How can they not realize that not all Muslims are Arabs when they have many Muslims here who are American?

GERMANY: American students are much more ignorant of other countries and cultures. I suppose it's because it's so big, and knowing about California for you is like us knowing about France. It's a neighbor. The U.S. is less dependent on other cultures, and maybe that's why they need to know less. Still, Americans come across as not interested in other cultures, like they don't really care about other countries. So they think things like Swedish people are only blonds.

INDIA: Somebody asked me if we still ride on elephants. That really bothered me. If I say I'm Indian, they ask which reservation? I say I'm from Bombay. "Where is Bombay?" Some people don't even know where India is. A friend of mine and I tried to make these Americans see what it was like and we asked them where they're from. They said California. And we said, Where was that?

FRANCE: People here don't know where anything is. For World War II, the teacher had to bring in a map to show where Germany and England are—it was incredible! I read somewhere a little research that said only 15 to 20 percent of Americans between the ages eighteen to twenty-five could point out Iraq on a map. The country will go to war, but it doesn't know where the country is!

Despite the critical consensus in these comments, it would be unfair of me to represent international student perspectives as roundly negative. In general, students from outside the United States warmly appreciated the American educational system as well as the spirit of the American college student. The criticisms that they did have, though, were pointed and focused. Taken together, they amounted to nothing less than a theory of the relationship among ignorance, intolerance, and ethnocentrism in this country, one that international eyes saw bordering on profound self-delusion. When I asked the linked questions, "What would you want American students to see about themselves?" and "What advice would you give them?" one German student stated succinctly what many students communicated to me at greater length: "Americans seem to think they have the perfect place to live, the best country, the best city. I hear that all the time. I used to think you just got that from politicians, but now I see it's from regular people too. The patriotism thing here really bothers me."

It is sobering to hear these words from a German student, whose country's historical experience in the 1930s and 1940s taught him the dangers of hypernationalism. To his fellow U.S. students he offered this recommendation: "I'd give them advice to live elsewhere. They should recognize that the way of living in the U.S. is fine, but it isn't necessarily the best way for everyone. I don't like to evaluate, and I'd like that applied to me. Be more informed. Information leads to tolerance."

It bothered a Chinese student who read in an article that American students don't want to study a foreign language because they believe that the world language will be English. "I think they need to learn about the world, to learn a foreign language," he urged. It bothered a British student, who lamented how much of world music American students seem to miss. "Everything here [on his corridor] is either black gangster rap or punk rock, and that's basically it. They don't want to hear other music—contemporary music from around the world."

The connection between lack of information and intolerance translated occasionally into personal stories of frustration, hitting home in the lives of some students. "I wish they [his hall mates] were accepting of more different music," said an Indian student. "I play my own music. I play it loud just like they do—

Arabic and Punjabi and other stuff—and they complain to the RAs. But it's my right to play that too. Why don't they understand that?"

"They don't accept other cultures," speculated one Japanese student.

> Once I was eating the food I had made—Japanese noodles—and we Japanese eat noodles with a noise. Somebody else in the kitchen area looked at me funny. She asked, "Why are you making so much noise?" I told her that's the way Japanese eat their noodles, and I can see by her face that she is disapproving. It hurt me to see that. Some Americans don't care about other worlds.

One key toward creating a more positive cycle of information, self-awareness, and tolerance was for many the university and university education itself. Learn a foreign language and study overseas, many recommended for individual students. Use your education to expand your purview beyond your own country. For the university, other students recommended a greater emphasis on self-awareness, including a more critical eye directed to our own institutions and history.

For one Chinese student, the need to be more reflective about the media representation of news and issues was critical: "Media coverage has a very great influence here. In China, it has less influence because everyone knows it's propaganda. Here it is not seen that way because there is a free press. But it's curious." In American newspaper articles and TV news, "the individual facts are true often, but the whole is not sometimes. I can see how Americans need to question the way stories are being represented to them."

A French student beseeched us to examine our own educational system:

> Americans teach like the only important thing is America. There is no required history course in college. The history course I took on Western civ. at AnyU was middle-school

level, and it was very biased. I mean they taught how, in World War II, America saved France and saved the world, how they were so great. The courses don't consider what Americans have done wrong. All the current events here is news about America and what America is doing. If it's about another country, it's about what America is doing there. There's nothing about other countries and their histories and problems. [In France] we had lots of history and geography courses, starting very young. I learned about France, but then we had to take a course in U.S. industrialization, in China, Russia, Japan, too. We got the history and geography of the world, so we could see how France now fits into the bigger picture.

For the international students I interviewed, American college culture is a world of engagement, choice, individualism, and independence, but it is also one of cross-cultural ignorance and self-delusion that cries out for remediation. It was a Somali student who summed up all of their hopes for "America": "You have so much here, and so many opportunities. I wish America would ask more what this country can do to make the world a better place."

CHAPTER 5

Academically Speaking . . .

There is an exercise I sometimes do in my large introductory anthropology classes in a unit on witchcraft to show how accusations in a culture can operate to reinforce unconscious social norms. I tell students there is one witch in the room who is responsible for all the bad things happening to them in the class. This witch, I explain—who could be either male or female—is the reason why some people in the class have colds, others feel sleepy in class, and still others have trouble taking the tests. The students laugh, knowing I'm just joking with them. "Whatever you think about the reality of witches," I continue, "I want you to take out a piece of paper and identify three people in the room who could be the potential witch."

The classrooms, which seat about one hundred people, are tiered lecture halls with chairs that are fixed in place. Students don't generally know the names of more than a few others in the class, so I have each student stand briefly and slowly state his or her first name and last initial. The other students listen and write down potential candidates for their list until everyone in the class has individually stood and stated his or her name. I then ask the students to narrow their list to three people and turn it in, which they do with chuckles as they leave the classroom.

Before the next class, I tally the results. Invariably, and much to the surprise of the class when I announce the numbers, the accusations converge on a few key individuals (whom I identify, if they have given me advance permission). "How could this be so?" I ask the class, emphasizing that we neither know other students personally nor believe in witchcraft.

After years of doing this, I find that students invariably pick the people whom I, as the teacher, would label the most engaged and prepared, if not the best students. They are the ones who ask me questions and respond to my questions, who come to class a little early or stay a little late, and who sit in the "reverse T" from my line of sight, that is, in the front row or two or in the center column of the classroom.

After a lively discussion, it becomes clear to the students that they hold largely unconscious norms about classroom behavior that focus on "equality," that is, on the importance of being the same as other students—one of "us." Aligning with authority by being too close in proximity or sensibility to the professor is suspect, as are students who are particularly vocal and regularly answer questions or make comments. Equality in the classroom usually amounts to "invisibility"; don't be too noticeable is the rule, whether that means acting like an outstanding student or a troublemaker. It is fine to do well in a class, performing better than others, but only if you do it unobtrusively.

As a student, I experienced the reality of these norms in a palpable way—one of the tangible advantages of the participant-observation research technique. I truly felt uncomfortable sitting too close to the professor, or letting my classmates think I was talking with him or her personally about non-class business; I noticed the subtle distance that making too many comments in class could create, although as an older student I had considerably more leeway and frequently violated the norms in a couple of classes where the lethargy was too deadly.

From my seventh-row seat in a large lecture hall, I could see the glances exchanged between fellow students when a notoriously vocal student in the first row would either ask the teacher for additional information or inject new information: "If you don't think this technology will last, could you tell us what you think will replace it?" asked one young man. I remember thinking to myself that he would be a good candidate for the witch in my own course (even if, with my teacher's gaze, I so appreciated this student).

A good question, I learned, is one that voices a concern shared by other students or that asks for clarification of upcoming work. "Will there be more questions on the test from the text or the lecture?" "Should the paper be double- or single-spaced?" A list of all questions asked by students on the first day in my five classes showed strict adherence to these classroom question norms (with only one exception), including inquiries such as these:

"What will be the form of exams?"
"Are the quizzes on the Internet?"
"Can we access quizzes beforehand?"
"Will the final paper be informational or persuasive?"
"What is the minimum number of sources that should be on the final paper?"
"Do you want the first essay typed?"
"Do we have to do the questions for next time?"
"Do you want a written answer to the questions?"[1]

One particularly sensitive community college professor told me, "I never use professional jargon in my classes, because if my students didn't understand what I was saying, no one in the class would ever ask me." As a student, I realized that he was right. "What does that mean?" is, incredibly, just not the kind of question that an American college student would ask.

Conventions of the Classroom

The typical course of forty or fewer begins in the same way. Students are expected to introduce themselves by going around the room and giving their first name, along with some other piece of identifying information. This ranged from lackluster offerings such as one's major or hometown to icebreaker exercises in which students respond to personal queries such as "My favorite food is————" or "A word I use to describe myself is————." Between preview activities, dorm meetings, and my five classes, I must have done this exercise close to a dozen times by the end of the first two weeks of school. It was what anthropologists would term a ritual.

Throughout the world, rituals accomplish different ends, but they often intensify social bonds and reiterate the values of a group. Singing the national anthem at ballgames is one such American ritual. It bonds spectators together in a shared tradition and reaffirms their common commitment to country. While the obligatory class introduction ostensibly serves to introduce, it also serves a much wider ritual function: it attempts to establish the perception of the classroom (or the dorm, or the Previews group) as a community. In round-robin introductions, everyone contributes, each person talks in turn, and everyone says something personal, reinforcing what the French anthropologist Hervé Varenne would characterize as the shared American ideal of community: a place of equality, informality, intimacy, and reciprocity.

Despite the fact that classes rarely function as communities, this ideal is powerful within the American classroom—at least for teachers. A good class is often thought of as one in which students speak repeatedly, and the teacher's role, as Varenne noted for the American high school, focuses on the elicitation and clarification of each student's viewpoint. These conventions, in fact, are built in to student evaluations of faculty. Was the class "open"? Did the instructor create an atmosphere in which you felt you could express your opinion?

In two of my classes teachers also handed out printed agreements for us to sign, laying out how we would interact, including pledges to "speak in turn," not interrupt one another, nor raise our voices or make personal comments. The assumption was that the agreement, which would be enforced by the teacher, would keep class discussion fair and civil by preventing students from becoming emotionally carried away by the controversy at hand.

In actuality, though, the teacher's role was less often to referee fervent debates than to get people to speak at all. Many times in class I felt as if I were saving the teacher by finally responding to some question he or she was trying to get us to react to. Although occasionally a class discussion could get heated, it was much more common to see students who were uninterested in debating one another than to see students whose debates were out of control.

Perhaps as a result, the teacher-student interaction focused less on what students said than on getting them to say something. Many classroom conventions were directed toward the purpose of soliciting opinions: requiring discussion in small groups and then asking each group to present its conversation to the class; going around the room and having everyone make a comment; asking each student to pose a question which other students must answer; and the least favorite, calling a name and asking the tapped person a question.

In particular instances throughout the year, I asked students to reflect on our lack of class participation in a given course. The answers I received varied widely, claiming such reasons as peer pressure (read as a reluctance to alienate or agitate classmates), the power of the teacher, and the lack of personal interest or purpose. Here are a few examples:

"I'm not always too interested in the topic, especially in liberal studies courses."
"No one listens to each other anyhow."
"Opinions are personal. I don't feel everyone needs to know my business."
"Sometimes I don't talk because I don't want to appear stupid."
"I feel if I talk up a lot like I may be talking too much."
"I don't want people all upset with me if they don't agree."
"The discussions are too teacher-directed—everyone is just saying what the teacher wants to hear."
"When teachers ask questions, they're just fishing for some answer they want you to say. So what's the point?"

"What's the good of getting all worked up about something when no one is going to change their minds anyway?"

"There's never any real debate in most issues classes. From what I see, everyone ends up believing the same thing. There's basic consensus, so why argue?"

The variety of stated opinions coupled with the uniformity of behavior suggested to me that—as in the witchcraft example—this is one of those areas where "natives" may be unaware exactly *why* they do what they do. My asking seemed to promote after-the-fact explanations and rationalizations, and it also made me realize that this was likely an issue that I, through my teacher's eyes, considered much more important than most students did.

Nevertheless, I was struck by the realization that, despite official assertions about the university as a free marketplace of ideas, the classroom doesn't often work that way in practice. Ideas are rarely debated, and even more rarely evaluated. Most classroom discussion, when it does occur, could be described as a sequential expression of opinion, spurred directly by a question or scenario devised by the teacher, which is subject to little or no commentary.

Even campus activism had a similar tone. Walking from class to class some days, I would see printed signs—one staked in the ground every few yards—that confronted me along the path. "Women work more hours than men each week but their work is unpaid and unaccounted for." A few yards later I'd see, "A woman is sexually assaulted every two minutes in America," and then "Girls represent nearly 60% of children not in school." The signs would go on that way—just signs. I came to understand that a particular campus group had reserved the walking mall for a day or two to put on a program. Sometimes the posted signs would ask a question like, "Do you know what to wear when you make love for the first time?" A few yards later would be a picture of a man and woman in wedding clothes, and I'd know this was sponsored by a Christian group. Other times I'd see, "The USA has executed 8 juvenile offenders since 1990," and know that the next signs would be about children's rights.

It was notable to me that feminist and Christian and human rights groups all enlisted the same approach, and that these mall presentations were somehow part of campus culture. It was assertion without direct dialogue, an "in your face" argument without a real face at the other end.

The time before and after classes, when teachers were not within earshot, was instructive. It was a time for academic and social small talk, including stories about the recent weekend, the "fun" things that were done, or how tired or "wasted" the speaker was at the moment. Academic discourse was limited to a narrow sort of mutual questioning. "Did you do the reading for today?" and "Did we have anything due today?" were both common pre-class queries. Shared complaints about the way a course was going ("I can't believe he hasn't turned back either of our last two assignments") or the prospect of the upcoming class ("I hope he doesn't do that in-class writing thing again") were also heard. What wasn't mentioned struck me as significant. One would never hear, "Did you like that reading?" or "That paper assignment really made me think." It's not that students didn't like the reading or find the assignments provocative; it's just that these weren't acceptable or normative topics to introduce in informal conversation.

When academic assignments *were* mentioned, the discourse converged on a couple of main themes. Students either talked about reactions and comparisons of evaluations received ("How did you do on that paper?" "What did you put for number 19?" "Man, what does that guy expect?") or they focused on the effort or attention given to academic assignments—usually emphasizing the lack thereof ("I mean, I didn't know what he wanted—I just guessed and b.s.-ed my way through this"; "I was down in the city for the weekend and I was fucking drunk the whole time. Wrote this paper totally wasted at three in the morning"; "I couldn't believe I got an A—I hardly studied!").

I found the distinction between the last minutes of class and the first minutes after class especially poignant because it highlighted the conversational boundary between course/formal time and free/informal time. The contrast was glaring in one of my seminar classes, where the professor regularly goaded us into taking and defending "stands" on issues. We would occasionally engage in class debates (or at least multiple expressions of opinion) that seemed ready to spill over into the halls after class. The moment that we walked out of class, though, the subject at hand was abruptly dropped, as if the debate had only been part of a classroom performance.

The boundaries of discourse seemed clear. Outside the classroom, and outside of specific academically or professionally focused clubs or events, students just didn't appear to talk among themselves about the ideas presented in their classes or the issues of the day. The informal public spaces of the university—and much, I suspected, of the private space—was directed toward other topics.[2]

Dorm Talk

To investigate this idea further and double-check my own impressions, I collected some data. I asked students what they talked about among friends, and I also posted the question in four locations in women's bathrooms for anonymous comment: "What topics do you talk about, late night, with friends?" In addition, I conducted a mini-study of conversation in public spaces by choosing eight twenty-minute evening blocks of time on random nights in mid-semester to walk the twelve halls in my dorm.[3] I wrote down the subjects of snippets of conversation that I could hear in the public domain.

When questioned generally, students responded, as they did to Michael Moffatt in the 1970s, that they *did* talk about deeper and higher matters. The question about late-night conversations posted in the women's bathrooms yielded a variety of general answers, from "Everything under the sun," to "Whatever is on our minds," to "What don't we talk about?" Yet despite these claims of boundless conversational variety, of seventy-five responses I received mentioning eighty-eight specific topics, almost one-third of all discussion topics reported were about boys, meeting boys, and sex. Other frequently reported topics fell into the following categories, in order of their frequency of mention:

- bodies, bodily functions, and body image
- relationships and relationship problems
- one's childhood, personal history, and future
- TV, movies, games, and entertainment
- alcohol and drug experiences

Together these six topics represented three-quarters of all the topics reportedly discussed among friends.

Only four (or fewer than 5 percent) of all conversation topics reported were related to academic or professional life. Of these, one concerned "careers," one "school," and two were about professors (although these were in regard to "hot profs" and "evil profs," respectively). Eight responses fell into the category of "philosophy, religion, or life," including two mentions of talking generally about "life," three of spirituality or God (including one about witchcraft), and one mention of philosophy. It was interesting that of these eight responses, three had a qualifying phrase attached. For instance, one woman wrote that she talked about "what everything means" but then added in parentheses, "If we're drunk or stoned we try to be all deep." Another listed "religion and philosophy," adding, "and more dorky things." These were the only statements in the entire sample qualified in this way, and I interpret this to mean that the writers were responding to some tacit social knowledge that their stated topics represented deviations from convention that needed to be explained or framed.

Some of my late-night talk results are probably "gendered," in the sense that the topics of relationships and bodies are more likely to dominate women's conversations. Dorothy Holland and Margaret Eisenhart show convincing evidence that college women's social and emotional lives are "profoundly affected by their sexual attractiveness to men."[4] My data linking women's private conversations to the subjects of "boys," "relationships with boys," "sex," and "bodies"—not with careers or academics—fit disturbingly well with their analysis, even fifteen years later. The notions, however, that peer culture is of central importance and that, for most segments of the student community, academic life is tangential to or at odds with peer culture are consistent with every major study of college life.[5]

From my own mini-study of conversation in the halls, I learned that, although there was occasional talk about academics, it accounted for less than 5 percent of the total subjects I heard discussed. What's more, the academic talk that I heard was of the same ilk as pre-class conversation. In the dorms, though, where many of the inhabitants do not attend class together, the conversation topics ranged more widely, from "What did you put on the test?" to opinions of current classes and professors ("My Web course sucks"; "I love my———prof"; "I can't believe the amount of work I have in————") to personal stories associated with academic bureaucracy (a contested grade, an adviser problem, the details of after-class dealings with a professor). Virtually none of the talk, aside from out-of-class meetings for a group project or joint homework session, concerned either the substantive content of a class or any other topic that might be labeled academic or intellectual. Although my time sample is very limited, I never once overheard what I would term a political or philosophical discussion.

The only written comments related to academics that were posted on the doors of students in the hall were (1) an Albert Einstein quotation printed in big letters stating, "It is a miracle that curiosity survives formal education"; and (2) the question "Can you believe this?" written in marking pen atop a printout of a personal e-mail from a teacher in a large lecture course explaining that professors were required to post midterm grades, but since he didn't have enough work from the class to grade, he would give everyone a C. Understand, the teacher went on, that this is not your real grade, but a classful of Cs will help to make the college grading statistics appear rigorous while at the same time satisfy the bureaucratic requirement to report mid-semester grades.

These lone student postings echoed a familiar refrain: the stupidity of the educational bureaucracy and authority; disen-gagement from the formal structures and requirements of acad-eme. By contrast, the RA postings on the official hall bulletin board were replete with educational advice, and the quotations displayed through these formal channels were quite different, citing Thoreau ("The world is but a canvas to the imagination"; "It takes two to speak truth—One to speak, and another to hear") and Emerson ("A chief event of life is the day in which we have encountered a mind that startled us").

The contrast between the RA postings and the student post-ings mirrors the contrast between informal and formal talk, be-tween in-class and out-of-class discourse. The undergraduate worldview, as I came to understand it, linked intellectual mat-ters with in-class domains and other formal areas of college life, including organized clubs and official dorm programs. "Real" college culture remained beyond the reach of university institu-tions and personnel, and centered on the small, ego-based net-works of friends that defined one's personal and social world. Academic and intellectual pursuits thus had a curiously distant relation to college life.

Taken together, the discourse of academe, both in and out of classes, led me to one of the most sobering insights I had as a professor-turned-student: How little intellectual life seemed to matter in college. This is not to say that no one cared about her education or that everyone cut all his classes. Rather, what I ob-served was that engagement in the philosophical and political issues of the day was not a significant part of college student culture.

What You Really Learn In College

Not only did ideas and issues play a limited role in college life, but classes did too. While most students I interviewed readily admitted that they were in college to learn, they also made clear that classes, and work related to classes, were a minor part of what they were learning.

I asked students directly in both interviews and surveys, "What percentage of your college learning comes from classes, or from the readings, films, group work, and papers related to classes, versus what percentage is from outside of classes?" The median response of students polled was that 65 percent of learning occurs outside of classes and class-related activities while 35 percent occurs within. Non-class-related learning was reported as high as 90 percent for some, and very few students ranked class activities as constituting more than 50 percent of what they learned in college. The great majority of students saw elective social activities and interpersonal relationships as the main context for learning.

So, if college is not primarily about either intellectual ideas and issues or classes, then what *is* college for? Don't students come to college to learn? Is college for most students simply about getting a degree, as some cynics might suggest?

I decided to broach these subjects by asking students directly, but anonymously, whether, if given the chance, they would "take the degree and run." I posted this graffiti question: "Be honest. If the university would hand you a bachelor's degree right now, provided you paid for all your credits and left the dorms, would you take the degree and leave?

Thirty-eight women responded anonymously with written answers. Of these, eleven said they would pay for their degree and leave because of reasons such as "I want to start my life," "I miss my boyfriend," and "I'm ready to start teaching now." Two-thirds of the sample, however, would choose to stay in college and finish their degrees the old-fashioned way.

Their reasons for doing so, though, fell into distinct categories. Three had concerns about not learning enough to get a good job ("As nice as it'd be not taking classes, you'd be out of luck when it comes to finding a job"; "Only if the degree came with all the knowledge I'd need for my career"). Three others located their discomfort in the American work ethic ("If it was handed to me, it wouldn't be the same as if I knew I was the one that worked hard to get what I deserved") or work's connection to the value of the degree ("No, then everyone would have a degree and its value would be set for a price—not awarded"). Only five students (13 percent of the entire sample, and 20 percent of the "No, I wouldn't take the degree" vote) mentioned directly the importance of education for its own sake ("What's the point of learning new things if ya don't get to learn them?").

By far the most compelling reason given for staying in college was "the college experience"—the joys and benefits of living within the college culture rather than in the real world. Thirteen students, representing more than half of the students who said they wouldn't just take the degree, made comments that fell into this category. Here are some examples:

"Who wants to be in the real world anyway?"
"No, because I would miss out on all the new friendships, all the partying, and all the late night talks with the homegirls. An experience one can't miss—Sorry."
"No way! Why try to live in the real world before I have to. Classes are a small price to pay."
"I want to stay as long as I can."
"Except for those pesky classes [smiley face], why would I ever leave this life of friends and fun?"
"The life experience is worth it."
"No, if I took the paper [diploma] all the fun would have to stop."
"No, college is too fun. Granted classes get in the way a bit but it's all worth the experience! I'm having a blast."

The biggest attraction of college for these students was clearly "college culture," which, consistent with the findings in this chapter, seemed to have very little to do with either intellectual life or formal instruction. Only one comment included a positive mention of classes, and even in this, the reference was parenthetical: "Why would I want to give up all the fun of college life (including classes) for a free ride?" Classes, in fact, were described in multiple instances as the "price one has to pay" to participate in college culture, a domain that students portrayed in terms such as "fun," "friendships," "partying," "life experiences," and "late night talks."

The Perfect Class

The tiny place occupied by anything academic in college life was a consistent message. This was disconcerting to me as a professor because I have always shared the professor's worldview that what we do is regularly mind-altering and life-changing. Surely, I thought, there are many courses that truly "make a difference" in students' lives, and as a student, I decided it was important to sample one of them personally. So I asked upperclassmen to advise me as a freshman: "Is there any class you've taken that really made a difference for you, and that you think I shouldn't miss at this university?" Much to my delight, three different students mentioned the same course and several more reinforced its reputation, affirming that "you've got to take this!" So I registered for the course—"Sexuality"—preparing myself to experience my fellow students' idea of the "perfect" class.

The first day of class felt like an underground meeting. There was excitement, and animated talking and laughing, as twelve "peer teachers," who would serve as our discussion leaders, sat with legs dangling over the edge of a stage. They faced us, the 250 or so students waiting for class to begin, with an air of confidence and esprit de corps. As we sat in the lecture hall, it was announced that those still hoping to get in should write a personal statement about why they wanted to be in the class and pass it forward. The rest of us felt lucky to be registered for the course.

We soon saw that this was no ordinary class. The middle-aged professor strode into the room late, like a rock star, as students waited in anticipation. His course introduction, like his lectures to follow, was peppered with taboo words and intimate personal stories. After the first two mentions of "fucking," the nineteen-year-old next to me whispered, "This guy is so cool!" The syllabus, which was passed conventionally in stacks through the aisles of students, soon sent up a murmur of incredulity because its front cover consisted entirely of an explicit (and funny) sexual cartoon about bestiality. The readings list included two books of erotica—"Hurry and buy them before other students scoop them up," we were warned—in addition to a standard human sexuality textbook. More than forty popular movies on video (from *When Harry Met Sally, 9½ Weeks,* and *Who's Afraid of Virginia Woolf,* to *The Crying Game* and *The Adventures of Priscilla, Queen of the Desert*) were listed as those we could watch at home and summarize for extra credit.

Then there were personal testimonies. Each of the peer teachers, who were to lead individual discussion groups, stood up and told a story about personal sexual transformation and how this course had changed his or her life. The stories were so graphic and intimate that the students were transfixed, not a sound in the room. "These students are modeling," we were told, "what you will be sharing in your small groups. Be open, honest, confidential, and you will learn. You will also make deep friendships within your groups that, based on what past students have told us, will last throughout your college years."

The small discussion groups (of which there were more than twenty-five) became the locus where, we were assured, the "real course" took place. We were told to meet off-campus, at a private residence if we could, because there had been complaints lodged from dorms and public establishments about the prurient nature of overheard conversations. There we were to share our personal histories, our sexual questions, issues, and advice, and our individual reactions to the readings and films. This was the only part of the course at which attendance was mandatory and where we would be literally counted.

An antiestablishment, edgy feel was a consistent theme within the class, despite the fact that weekly lectures were pretty standard and the bulk of the course grade consisted of two multiple-choice exams, with questions gleaned from lectures, films, and readings. When we arrived in class most weeks, we would find flyers from local pubs and dance clubs placed unofficially on our chairs. As part of our two-and-a-half-hour lecture period each week, we were regularly shown provocative films—on homosexuality, masturbation, elder sex, female dominance. Classroom doors were conspicuously shut, amid student tittering, and the screening would be prefaced with a description that included a rating from 1 to 10 for the film's shock content.

Students continually reproduced the aura of being "out there," both internally within the course and for those outside the class. The internal dialogue was most apparent at the breaks between film and lecture segments, when we listened to announcements, both bland and provocative, made by the peer teachers: "Group 19, remember to meet at Howie's house, not Jean's, next week," or "Group 5, those going on the Las Vegas trip, meet in the parking lot of the Union on Saturday." There was always a buzz from the lecture hall over each risqué-sounding field trip, just as a shriek of laughter would greet the announcement, "The group—we won't say the number—that got itself busted in the hotel hot tub should be more discreet in the future." Announcing the past and planned exploits of the groups became almost a competition, and part of course culture. My own small group (Group 8) petitioned our peer teacher to make the bogus announcement before the whole class that "Group 8 members should make sure they have their passports ready for the trip."

In the end, I saw the worth of this course, as well as its student appeal. The "perfect" class may not have been perfect from an academician's point of view, but it melded the presentation of ideas, information, and theory (about one-third of class content) with essential components of undergraduate culture, including the drama of interpersonal relations, a sense of rebellion and irreverence, and a small interactive community, enforced by a weekly attendance rule.

"Sexuality" was the quintessential college course because it reflected most students' view of what they really learn in college, as well as the proportion of social versus academic content that they believed their learning to comprise. It subsumed formal academic content within an informal, largely social world characterized by equality, informality, intimacy, and reciprocity, while at the same time it provided a context for learning that was "fun," irreverent, and separated, both geographically and ideologically, from the formal aspects and authority of campus.

CHAPTER 6

The Art of College Management

I t is always dangerous to view our collective lives without the benefit of history or without regard to diversity among us. In interpreting all I have described so far about the college scene and college student, the reader must bear two insights in mind. The first—lest one become too perturbed by "today's youth" and their anti-intellectualism—is that at least some of these dynamics are two centuries old. College student culture has long had its own rules that kept professors, classes, and intellectual life at arm's length. The second salient point to remember is that not all college students buy into the dominant paradigm of the day. College culture, like any culture, is neither singular nor monolithic. There are subcultures and alternative cultures that have long existed within American colleges and universities. They still do.

In the next few pages I rely heavily on Helen Horowitz's historical text *Campus Life* to introduce the cultural traditions of the college campus. This brief overview offers a context for interpreting the details and dynamics of contemporary college life, both what I have presented so far and what I describe in this chapter.

"Classic" American college culture, which developed as early as the eighteenth century, arose out of elite male experience. For these students, it was relationships with their wealthy peers—not teachers—that would form the important personal networks in their college and post-college life. Fraternities and sports clubs, purveying values of exclusivity, hedonism, and adolescent rebellion, were the locus of early college life. As Horowitz notes, "the real measure of success was the judgment of peers"; although intelligence was valued, it was judged by student standards rather than by the grades or accolades proffered by the faculty. Since students' relationships with professors were often openly adversarial, there was no premium on getting to know faculty members inside or outside of class. Indeed, students who sought teacher contact and approval became the objects of scorn or ridicule.[1]

These cultural codes of old expressed themselves in ways very similar to the student culture of the twenty-first century: resistance to speaking in class; social distance from faculty; a "code of honor" that included silence about cheating, drinking, and other infractions; and a hedonistic emphasis on fun, sex, and alcohol as markers of the real "college experience." This comment from an early-twentieth-century collegian reflecting on his undergraduate experience is practically indistinguishable from rules of classroom interaction as I experienced and recorded them in 2003: "It was sticking your neck out if you spoke up in class and answered a professor's question to the group as a whole. It was likewise regarded as bad form to do reading for the course above and beyond the assignment and to let that be known."[2]

Alternative models of student culture became prominent as "outsiders"—Jews, women, and, later, people of color and immigrants—entered college in larger numbers.[3] These students, often from poor backgrounds, worked harder than other students and developed reputations as "grinds" who stayed aloof from the clubs and sports of college life, which rejected them anyway. For these students, school was a more precious opportunity than for the male elite, as well as a gateway to the professions. "Outsiders" valued intellectual discourse, had a respect for good grades, and cultivated close relationships with faculty.

"Rebels"—who dominated the college scene in the 1960s and 1970s, but also during the postwar 1940s and 1950s—offered an alternative model. They repudiated traditional beliefs and authority as they rejected classic college life. Rebels' nonchalance about grades prevented their being used as leverage, and these students regularly leveled challenges to pedagogical values, administrative policy, and academic thought.

At AnyU these cultural archetypes remain recognizable. The Greek system, which still typifies many features of traditional college life, contrasts sharply with the studious, serious approach to academics I witnessed among international students, one modern version of outsiders. Religious, ethnic, sexual, and gender identity form the basis for core cohorts that enliven and politicize the life of the contemporary university. Functioning often as "rebels," and sometimes as "outsiders," these cohorts frequently find academic homes in women's studies and ethnic studies departments, in student organizations such as the Black Student Union, and in campus churches. By associating with those of like mind, these students find respite from the dominant pushes and pulls of college life. They can be observed contesting the academic status quo from both the left and the right.

On campuses today, neither the rebels nor the outsiders can compete with the form of student culture that burgeoned in the 1970s, what Horowitz labeled the "new outsiders": "The psychology of the New Outsider is more complicated than that of the college man. Nineteenth-century collegians owed individual professors respect, but could openly scorn them as a class. College men controlled the allocation of status because they chose those who led in sports and clubs. In the late twentieth century, professors hold the one judgment that matters to the New Outsiders—grades."[4] The new outsiders are practical and careerist in their approach to education, often showing little interest in the extracurriculum apart from professional club activities that bolster their résumé; the degree is seen primarily as a ticket to a better job rather than a better mind. Their interest in grades leads to close surface connections with faculty, while, like some earlier student cultures, they harbor a private disdain for the professoriate and the unworldly intellectualism of the liberal studies curriculum.

Students I met on campus were drawn from all four cultural archetypes, and some recognized themselves as more closely aligned with one or the other. Punks, goths, nerds and geeks, skaters, preps, Christians, freaks, Greeks, granolas: these are just a few of the labels students apply to distinguish "types" and approaches to university life. Still, despite the diversity, a dominant model exists on campus, and those who don't fit must contend with their own differentness. Some new rebels, including environmentalists and feminists, decry the lack of social and political consciousness on campus, just as real outsiders, perhaps evangelical Christians and "granolas" alike, balk at the role of alcohol in college life.

Although I stop short of naming the dominant model, because it seems an amalgam of at least "classic" and "new outsider" traditions, it is no less real for the lack of a label. The themes that pervade college life and the matters that concern college students are inescapable when you are living them. History may provide a useful lens through which to interpret what we see. I turn now to consider how students at AnyU negotiate their lives at college so you, my readers, can make your own judgments about the model of campus life that now predominates.

From Time Management to College Management

I cannot overemphasize the attention that "time management" receives in college preparation rhetoric today. Time management was the subject of entire workshops during both my Previews weekend and Welcome Week; it was a central topic when, as freshmen, we were invited to "Meet the Dean" of a college, and then again when we attended an advising seminar. These presentations offered students consistent advice and a uniform viewpoint on college life and success that went something like this: College is demanding, but you don't need to be a drudge. The key to succeeding at college is effort and good planning. If you plan your time well, you can have it all.

The dean dove into the trenches with us, outlining on a blackboard every hour of our 24/7 week. Allowing us 8 hours of sleep per night, he explained, we had 168 hours at our disposal, if we didn't fritter away our time. After subtracting the time necessary for eating, grooming and dressing, and traveling to class, the dean then allotted us 15 hours of in-class time and a recommended 30 hours of out-of-class time—two for every class hour—for studying, reading, homework, writing papers, and reviewing notes. Since many students worked, he added 10 hours a week, the maximum he recommended, for our jobs. Even after joining the recommended professional and interest club activities, we would still be able to go out to a movie every week, he concluded triumphantly. No one expected Jill or Jack to be all work and no play. We could have a balanced social and academic life if we would just stay mindful of our time and not waste those minutes in between classes, before meals, and after the morning alarm.

In every "time" or "stress" workshop I attended, the leader recommended getting a day planner, which we were to use religiously to enter appointments, classes, study time, test times, and paper due dates. The planner would serve as a master schedule, allowing us to see what needed to be accomplished when. Clearly, the key to success was the careful management and control of our time (a.k.a. life).

There is some level at which this official assessment was accurate. Going to school, I found, was a time management nightmare; student life required much more and a very different kind of juggling than my life as a professor, even with its diverse service, teaching, and research demands. As a student, I was quick to learn, you serve many masters, each with his or her own quirks, schedules, and predilections.

In my first semester I took five courses with five different instructors. Two courses had some sort of discussion or lab requirement, each with its own teacher, and one course had an out-of-class tutor. This meant that in a single semester there were eight different people who made rules or created structures that I had to respond to as a student. Each wanted us to access readings, or prepare papers, or communicate with him or her according to a different protocol. As is typical in a large state university, none of the instructors coordinated assignments or schedules with one another or even with a master university schedule.

Hence, office hours were posted for each professor based on personal schedules and preferences; university events such as Honors Week and department and program offerings regularly conflicted with one another and with club and class schedules. The university had designated no unscheduled hours during the week when meetings, lectures, film series, or other events could be held without interference. So attending a special film showing, or taking a class field trip, or even getting to a professor's office hours often meant sacrificing some other commitment.

You would not know until you put all your dates and deadlines into your day planner how many papers were due in the same week, or how many tests fell on the same day as the Halloween party. Even with the planner, you could not predict whether the homework demands in a given week would exceed the time available; any kind of spontaneity threatened to thwart the best-laid plans.

I found that I needed not only a day planner and a large erasable calendar to arrange my week but also the counsel of some savvy upperclassmen who had figured out how to deal with the diverse and unpredictable demands on a college freshman. Fellow students taught me the limitations of the administrative outlook on college success. It is not that the time management strategies proffered by the administration are wrong; they're just misplaced in emphasis. Many of the academically most successful juniors and seniors I interviewed believed that they did, indeed, need to control their time to create a balanced life.

What they had figured out, however, was that one could not or would not do this simply by "grinding" and jumping through the academic hoops of five to eight professors in each of sixteen semesters. The key to managing time was not, as college officials suggested, avoiding wasted minutes by turning yourself into an agent of your day planner. Neither was it severely curtailing your leisure or quitting your paying job. Rather, it was controlling college by shaping schedules, taming professors, and limiting workload.

Shaping Semesters: The Perfect Schedule

The shift in thinking from managing time and self to managing college means, first of all, that schedules will not shove you around, pulling you out of bed in the early morning and causing you to run back and forth across campus or unnecessarily chop up chunks of free time. Controlling time means consciously designing blocks of time during the week that are unscheduled by external demands, during which one can exercise one's right to socialize, travel, sleep, party, and/or work. This excerpt from an undergraduate advice article on one institutional Web site nicely encapsulates the "native rules" for formulating the perfect class schedule:

1. Don't take early classes, defined as "anything before 11 A.M."
2. Don't take classes on Friday, defined as "the day after Thursday but before Saturday."
   Point No. 2 is important because in college, weekends last at least three or four days, and Thursday sort of becomes the new Friday. Unless you're in a fraternity or sorority, in which case weekends last six or seven days.
3. Don't take any class with an unknown professor, defined as "a professor whom you know nothing about." . . . Having the right prof, many times for the exact same class, can mean the difference between Easy Street and Countless Hours of Pointless Busywork Street. The latter of which could seriously cut into your sleeping.[5]

While it may seem simple to schedule courses Monday through Thursday (some students even aim for a more refined Monday/Wednesday or Tuesday/Thursday schedule), scheduling is in fact an art—perhaps even a science.

This is because, however convenient your schedule, it must also get you into required courses, or courses that apply within a mandatory block requirement (such as humanities or sciences). If possible, your schedule should also keep you in the right geographic location so that your Spanish course, which ends at 9:50, is not at the other end of campus from your business course, which begins at 10:10. It also must hook you up with the "right" professor, as indicated in rule 3, and offer you a set of courses that promises to deliver a reasonable workload.

Around registration time, there is a spate of information exchanges concerning professors and courses and centering on workload. It was during this time that I asked students to identify their best course and their worst course for the past semester, with some indication of why, "because we're about to register for classes and opinions help!" A definite theme that emerged in these student-to-student recommendations was an affirmation of "easy" courses and "easy As", as indicated in these comments:

"Take Professor Jones, the man to see when you need an 'A.'"
"Don't take 302 with Smith because you can't understand what he wants you to know and he doesn't give As."
"I loved 101. It was sooo fun! And sooo easy!"
"Need to boost your GPA? Take 242."
"145 sucks. Never *take* it. You do three times the amount of work for the same credits and lower grades."
"Sign up for 235. The course is boring but it's easy as hell, and there's tons of extra credit."
"Take 298, it's sooo easy."

The clear emphasis on undemanding courses and work-free As must, however, be understood in a larger context. Workload considerations require a global, almost god's-eye view of one's life and purpose. What balance of papers and tests can one handle in a single semester? What painless course can one take to counter the killer required math course or the paper-heavy women's studies elective? What interesting, perhaps even challenging courses can one take without ruining one's cumulative grade point average?

The mature, thoughtful student needs to know the "easy As" so he or she can supplement a schedule that already contains heavy course loads or demanding classes. Thus, students also recommended a few courses that were "hard" or "challenging" but interesting; one student reacted to the final comment on the list ("Take 298, it's sooo easy"), querying, "Isn't college supposed to be challenging?" The response came back: "You have to have some easy courses so you don't get burned out." In light of my interviews with other students, this is a fairly accurate encapsulation of how workload is figured into scheduling. It's all a question of balance.

Producing one's final schedule is ultimately a matter of weighing considerations of interest, time, and requirements with the multiple sections of posted course offerings. Figuring out the right combination of locations, times, course subjects, workloads, and professors is like fitting a giant jigsaw puzzle together. A piece may look as if it fits—it gets exciting—but at the last moment you realize that the lab, which must be taken with the ideal course selection, meets only on Friday afternoon, or at the same time as a required course in your major. Even worse is when the entire schedule works but the last course to be fit into the schedule is full.

To avoid such a catastrophe, savvy students try to be the first to register. At AnyU, as at most universities, there is a seniority system for registration: seniors are allowed to register first, followed by juniors, then sophomores, then freshmen. Within these ranks, students can register on-line on a first come–first served basis; the beginning of registration was the only time I ever saw juniors wake at 5 AM (when registration access opened). Skilled undergrads have carefully laid out their preferences and are poised to enter their course choices as quickly as possible into the computer.

Even with all this effort, many students still do not get into every course in their well-crafted schedules. Then there is scrambling: "Does anyone know of an open Tuesday/Thursday 11:15 class that fits into the social science block?" It suddenly became clear to me why, as a professor, I had had a number of students enrolled in my basic cultural anthropology course who had no idea what anthropology was. My course was likely the last piece in their scheduling puzzle, and frankly, they didn't care what anthropology was.

It also became apparent why Web courses have become so popular among undergraduates living on college campuses, despite the fact that they were initially developed for place-bound individuals who could not come to campus.[6] On-line courses are the panacea not just for the place-bound but for the time-bound as well. Although their academic reputation is quite variable, and many students complained about their Web course experiences, on-line courses are the great scheduling "wild card." Because classes don't physically meet, and one can turn in assignments on-line at 3 AM, they fit into any work and course schedule and often become the ace in the hole that saves a perfect schedule from obliteration.

When all else fails, the final strategy when the "perfect" class has no more seats is to convince the professor that you should receive an override into the class. This shifts the focus of attention from schedule management to professor management.

The Care and Handling of Professors

There is only a slight difference between the rhetoric of pleasing one's professor, which surfaces in many formal advising venues, and "playing" one's professor. In its more thinly veiled forms, students are given advice like this, which appeared in the dorms on RA bulletin boards touting helpful academic hints:

"Get to know your professors. Your professors are much more understanding when they know who you are. This is helpful when there is a family emergency or when you get sick."

or

"Go to class, and talk to your profs. Professors are notorious for giving hints in a conversation that can help you on tests, such as 'this is very important.'"

or

"Sit in the front, so profs can see you. They won't know you if they can never see you. And they won't help you if they don't know you."

Even official university spokespersons tout similar advice. At one university-sponsored presentation for freshmen, the speaker advised us to sit in the "reverse T" (the center of the room or front row), in the professor's field of vision. An entire section of the talk was devoted to "Figuring Out Your Profs." It sounded like a lesson in corporate negotiation. "What do you want from profs?" the speaker asked. The answer, gleaned from the student audience, was this: career advice, information, recommendations, and As. What do profs want? The speaker told us: "They think the world revolves around their subject, so they want you to get it. They want to see effort, and they want you to voice an opinion. So give them what they want and you'll get what you want too!"

There is little mention, officially or unofficially, of learning or discovery in any of this rhetoric about students and professors. The advice given consistently suggests that the student-professor relationship should be understood in an instrumental way: You can get what you want from classes by establishing and using a personal relationship with your teachers.

These same precepts are reflected in the way many successful students talk about their own academic performance, and in their reflections on why they excel in school. Several of the undergraduates whom I as a fellow student admired most cast professor-student relations as a rough facsimile of the boss-worker relationship.

Consider this advice from one competent and mature senior when I asked what made her so successful as a student,

I take the information I need from the professor—how they're going to grade you and what they think is important—and I use it. If you write what you want to that prof, you're gonna end up with a bad grade. Whereas, if you write to *them*, you win—you can still have your own mindset and say, hell, I know this isn't the way I feel, but I'll give them what they want.

Another student responded: "How do I deal with teachers? I'm friendly with them. I ask them about their weekend and tell them about mine. They're just people. If they like you and you need a favor or have a problem, they'll be more likely to resolve it in your favor."

It was my impression that neither of these students viewed his attitude as manipulative or insincere; they were just, from their point of view, being realistic and mature about how to deal with different personalities who have power over you. Perhaps their outlook explains the national data, which show that, as students continue through their undergraduate years, they not only ask more questions in class but also report speaking to teachers more outside of class.[7] Although one could attribute this difference to increased interest in classes or improved self-confidence, I think it is at least partially explained by the advice proffered by successful students, resident assistants, and university representatives about creating and using relationships with professors.

This relationship advice, however, has its cultural sticking points. While it fits nicely with a careerist cultural outlook that privileges grades and degrees, it rubs against more classic college precepts that frown on treating professors like buddies. I saw this tension at work at AnyU. Even though there are still strong conventions against being publicly "chummy" with professors, many students seem to implement discreetly the advice to "be friendly to your professors." As a result, there is a sort of duplicity—a public versus a private face—built in to the student-teacher interaction, a product of its own internal conflicts, which contemporary undergraduate culture promotes and reproduces.

Controlling college life, though, is only partially advanced by a well-chosen, well-oiled professor or a perfect schedule. In the end, you must find ways to limit your workload by containing the amount of time you devote to any given course.

Limiting Workload: Doing What's Necessary

A common way to regulate workload is simply to restrict the amount of time and effort one spends on a course by doing no more than is necessary. On several levels, students assess what is needed to get by. Depending on the course and the instructor, they decide whether to buy the book, whether to go to class, whether to do the readings in a given week, and how much effort to put into assignments.

Attendance. The advice given by administrators, teachers, and students alike is that "you have to be there." The first rule for college success is "go to class." The reason this bromide appeared so frequently on dorm bulletin boards and elsewhere is that many students don't. Even though seasoned students recommend against it, cutting or "ditching" class is a strategy adopted by a number of students to free up more time in their lives.

Most successful students do not undertake this strategy too frequently or without regard to the class. Classes that require attendance as part of the course grade, and in which the instructor takes attendance, are rarely cut. By contrast, in classes where attendance is expected but not required, the frequency of absenteeism rises with each of the following characteristics: the class is large; the class is boring; tests are based on readings rather than lectures; grades depend on papers rather than tests; the class is early in the morning; the class in on Friday.

One of the more ditchable classes I attended was a large lecture course in which the professor presented what I considered to be interesting, beautifully organized, and up-to-date lecture material. An outline of lecture notes was organized into a booklet, which one could buy, so, as the teacher explained, it would not be necessary to scribble hurriedly all the concentrated information we received during each class period. The same professor taught multiple sections of the course, totaling 675 students, and had students sign in for each class, even though there was no attendance requirement. At the end of the term, I was able to get access to the attendance data for the course.

Fifty-six percent of students over the span of a semester came to class. To put it more accurately, classes were, on the average, 56 percent full. By no means was such a figure unusual, and this was an excellent class. I attended *many* classes in which substantial numbers of students were absent. On days before holidays, or days where there was great weather or bad weather, the empty seats were even more noticeable. In one period of the surveyed class, the teacher announced that, although testable material would not be covered in the next class period, she would be conducting an interactive experiential lesson that "would be very engaging." Eleven percent of the class showed up.

I found it particularly amusing that during the semester in this same class we received a university survey asking us to "self-report" on our attendance in that class in four categories:

How often do you come to class?

1. Less than 50% of the classes
2. 51–74% of the classes
3. 75–94% of the classes
4. 95–100% of the classes

Of the seventy-seven people in my section who responded anonymously, 90 percent, I found out later, reported that they came to 95–100 percent of the classes; only one person claimed to attend 51–74 percent of the classes, and none admitted attending fewer than 50 percent. Perhaps these self-reports were true, given that the survey was administered *in* class, but even so, I suspect that students either misperceived or misreported their actual behavior. In national surveys, one-third of students report skipping classes occasionally or more, a figure that my experience suggests is far too low, and almost two-thirds of students indicated that they sometimes came late to class.[8]

On the occasions when I, too, "ditched" a class, the reactions I received from other students were noticeably positive, including a "thumbs up" and an understanding "we all need a break" from hall mates, and "way to go, girl," from a classmate. Moderate cutting was part of college culture, and it marked me as one of them, as someone who understood the value of self-determination combined with a touch of rebellion. Still, the operative word is moderate. Ditching class was a minor time-saving (or week-shaping) strategy compared with limiting preparation.

Preparation. According to the 2003 National Survey of Student Engagement (NSSE), a survey of 437 colleges and universities in the United States, "only about 13% of full-time students spent more than 25 hours a week preparing for class, the approximate number that faculty members say is needed to do well in college. More than two fifths (41%) spent 10 or fewer hours a week."[9] The Higher Education Research Institute (HERI) survey of more than thirty thousand freshmen found that fewer than one-third of students spend even *one* hour studying or doing homework for every hour they spend in class.[10]

Given their work input, college students' grade performance nationwide is remarkable. According to national data, "more than three-quarters (77%) of all students who study 10 or fewer hours per week get a B or better."[11]

So, how do students do it? How do they manage to get by with less than half of the recommended preparation for class?

My answer is that good students have learned a kind of spartan efficiency. I learned it too. In the beginning of my first semester, I did all my readings when they were assigned. By the end of my first semester, I picked and chose, often relegating textbook reading to cram sessions during exam time, some-times skipping readings altogether. On papers, I cut my normal multiple revision process to just one draft and then a final paper. Even so, by peer standards I was practically a drudge.

Some of the biggest blocks of student leisure time are carved out of course preparation. Most commonly, students simply don't do the required readings for class. I'm not kidding. In cer-tain classes the professor would be lucky if one-third of the stu-dents read the materials at a level of basic comprehension.

National surveys support my personal observations. The NSSE found that 21 percent of college freshmen reported never having come to class without completing the readings or as-signments, which means that almost four-fifths of freshmen had. More telling, though, is the survey's comparison of fresh-men and senior self-reports. More seniors than freshmen report coming to class without completing assigned work: 82 percent of seniors said that they sometimes, often, or very often came to class without completing readings or assignments, up 2 percent or nearly two thousand students in the sample, from freshmen. This finding suggests something that I experienced more anec-dotally: that this kind of strategic corner-cutting is part of what students learn in college.

Students also skimp in other ways. Take Harry. He's a bright guy who works fifteen hours a week and plays an intramural club sport. His five classes include two in his major, one physi-cal education elective, and two liberal studies classes, including social science, in which the instructor assigns biweekly "thought" papers.

He usually does his social science homework, which is due on Thursdays, on Wednesday nights. But his team won this Wednes-day, and they went out for dinner, and then beers, and then more beers. He came home after 2 AM and set his alarm for 7:30 but didn't wake until 8. It took him twenty minutes to compose and print out the one- or two-page reflective essay due for class on his "experiences with and thoughts about race in America" (his was closer to one page) and ten minutes to wash and dress; he even had time to catch a quick breakfast before his 9:10 class.

Well over one-third of students in a national sample said that they had turned in course assignments that did not reflect their best work. Another 15 percent reported handing in course assignments late.[12] Low preparation time, as we have seen, is clearly a factor in producing less than high-quality work, but the reverse is true as well: low-quality work creates time, making room for other activities in one's schedule that have priority. It is this trade-off that I observed among fellow undergraduates: massive shortcuts—particularly in courses that a student considers "busywork" or irrelevant to his or her career—enabling students to shape their lives and their time more fully.

Thus, the commercial flyer handed out to us at an all-freshman seminar was well targeted: "Want good grades AND free time?" it read. It was selling an on-line bibliographic and database service for the stated goal, which appeared in big letters, of "Better papers, faster."

It is just a stone's throw from these observations to the next issue.

Cheating.   If you believe that cheating is simply a manifestation of individual morality, then the current data on student behavior lead to the conclusion that the majority of today's youth are amoral at best. The national literature is consistent and undeniable. College students cheat. At least half engage in serious cheating, more than two-thirds admit to cheating on a test, and more than three-quarters have cheated in some capacity.[13]

But looking at cheating as an individual character issue disregards the role of undergraduate culture. Although cheating has increased slightly, particularly in some key areas, it has figured prominently in all the years academics have measured it. In 1963 a national study determined that 81 percent of college students had engaged in some form of dishonest academic behavior; in 1993 the percentage was 83 percent. Cheating was an active part of classic college culture of the nineteenth and twentieth centuries and remains so in the twenty-first, as schools across the country report high levels of academic dishonesty.

In these excerpts from an on-line article, one can hear the contemporary tone regarding cheating. The article, "How to Master Test-Taking—Without Technically Cheating," makes clear that at least some forms of academic dishonesty in college culture are literally nothing to be ashamed of:

> Now this, understandably, is a bit of a thorny issue. Some parts will depend on your definition of cheating, other parts on whether you care if you cheat. And others still will depend on how great the lengths you'll go to in order not to get caught. But the key to the whole thing is understanding this: Practically every single class you'll take has already been taken by someone else. Think about what that potentially means. Besides, cheating is kind of like traveling in basketball or stealing signs in baseball—everybody does it.

The article goes on to advise, among other things, that students should locate others who have taken the course before and solicit copies of their old tests or their memories about test questions. "If none of this will fly," the author concludes, "good luck doing things the old-fashioned way. Your halo will arrive with your diploma, six to eight weeks after graduation."[14]

Cheating is a fascinating subject, because, from a student's as opposed to a teacher's vantage point, it has many subtleties and complexities. As the article suggests, cheating is like "stealing signs in baseball"—practically part of the game. It's really not that bad a thing, everyone knows you do it, and sometimes it is too much to your disadvantage not to do it.

Evidence from national studies suggests that an increasing number of students question whether certain behavior—such as getting questions from former students, as the article advises—qualify as cheating. Twenty-one percent of students nationally said they didn't consider copying from another student on a test or exam to be a serious cheating offense. Even more students questioned the seriousness of using crib notes

(23 percent), helping someone else cheat on a test (28 percent), and plagiarism (31 percent).[15]

I did not collect data on the frequency of cheating or admitted cheating, but I did ask fellow students about the idea of cheating. Like students across the country, most who spoke with me were well aware that cheating is rampant in college life. In studies, as many as 90 percent of college students reported seeing another student cheat in the previous year; the national average was 80 percent.[16]

Most students I questioned, though, did not support the general idea of cheating when it was understood as consistently gaining unfair advantage over classmates by engaging in dishonest academic behavior. At the same time, just as in national samples, they had serious questions about what really constitutes cheating and what does not. Isn't it OK to work on homework together? We don't have to cite other people's ideas on tests, so why is it cheating if we don't cite in papers? Is it really cheating to sign in a friend on an attendance roster? Moreover, the students recognized many circumstances that might justify a particular instance of cheating as well as gradations in behavior that would cause one to question the label of academic dishonesty.

In a posted query, I asked "(When) is it OK to cheat?" At least one-third of respondents said that it is never acceptable to cheat, but in response to the students who answered "never" were challenges like these:

"Oh come on. Don't you think that everyone has cheated at least once?"—damn, no one is a saint."
"Excuse me, but there are worse things to do than cheat on homework."
"Haven't any of you ever looked over just to see if the other person had the same answer as you. Yes, sometimes it's just reassurance."

Well over half of the students who responded thought that in some way or other, it really depends.[17]

On what, then, does cheating depend? In a policy-focused study at one North Carolina university, students offered reasons that they thought should be taken into consideration in disciplining students caught cheating. These were: (1) performance pressure, (2) personal problems that made it difficult or impossible to study, (3) unrealistic expectations from instructors, and (4) meaningless or irrelevant assignments.

Many of the answers I received at AnyU regarding situational justifications for cheating fell into similar categories, and then some.[18] By far the largest number of responses were related to items (3), which I will modify to read "unrealistic or *unfair* expectations from instructors *or the university*," and (4). Here are some samples of AnyU student responses to the posted question "(When) is it OK to cheat?"

"If you don't give a shit about the class but are required to take it and the info they are making you learn you know you won't ever use again."

"If it's on-line. On-line courses suck."

"When the info on the test/paper/homework is totally irrelevant!"

"When it's a liberal studies class that has no relevance to your major."

"If you studied but the test doesn't test what the instructor promised. As long as you learned the info, what's wrong with it?"

"When it pertains to absences. I cheat on absent slips. We pay to come to college—they shouldn't make us sign in for any class!"

These responses are consistent with research across the country, which shows that students increasingly find cheating more acceptable and justifiable. Donald McCabe and the Center for Academic Integrity have conducted national studies of academic honesty for more than 40 years. One of the most disturbing recent shifts, McCabe contends, is "the ease with which many of these students are able to justify or rationalize their cheating. And often they find a convenient way to place the 'blame' on others—other students who cheat; faculty who do a poor job in the classroom; institutions that don't try very hard to address the issue of cheating; and a society that supplies few positive role models when it comes to personal integrity."[19]

Although it is tempting to pin the reason for increased cheating on the character failings of students, I rely on a helpful concept that anthropologists employ when trying to understand other cultures: cultural relativism. In this view, the observer is entreated to withhold judgment and attempt to understand behaviors and customs within the framework of that culture's structures, values, and goals. In this way we avoid attributing realities that disturb us to evil people. In utilizing cultural relativism, I recite a mantra to myself: assume that people are alike (and overall decent) in their basic character. When trying to understand a strange or objectionable behavior, assume that you would do the same thing in that culture or those circumstances. Then explore why someone like you might behave as others behave.

Such an inquiry is aided, of course, by participant-observation research, and, indeed, I gained some added insight into student mindsets by walking in the shoes of a student. In one of my smaller classes I remember thinking how silly it was that another older student encircled her quiz papers with her arms so that those on either side couldn't see. In an act of unspoken solidarity with my classmates, who had become at least friendly acquaintances, I consciously left my test papers open to view. No one, to my knowledge, ever used them, but neither did I have any pressing interest in preventing it.

Although I never thought of myself as actually cheating (like many students on national surveys), there were two other incidents that would certainly qualify as such by national measures when I collaborated with another student on a homework problem or assignment that probably should have been done individually.

My own brief encounters with academic integrity convince me of the inadequacy of published characterizations, which typically emphasize the more dramatic and negative findings in national studies. Cheating must be interpreted in its lived contexts, and when it is, it can be said that most of the time, most students don't cheat. Seventeen percent of students are habitual test cheaters (defined as three or more self-reported incidents),[20] a statistic that offers a very different picture of the student body from reports highlighting the 83 percent of students who admit engaging in some dishonest act.

Moreover, some cheating seems impelled not by moral laxity but by competing cultural values, particularly those of classic college culture. While most students value honesty, they are reluctant to turn in another student for cheating (only 9 percent nationally say that they would) or turn down a classmate's request for help on the homework. The most frequent types of cheating include those that seem to value student mutual aid and reciprocity over scrupulousness: signing in a classmate for attendance; getting questions or answers from those who have taken a test; working on an assignment with others.[21]

Other examples of the most common forms of cheating involve buying time or cutting scholastic corners, such as making false excuses to gain extra time on tests or papers, adding phony bibliographic sources; and copying from a source into a paper without footnoting. While I can't condone many forms of academic dishonesty, selective cheating operates as one in a larger set of related behaviors that give students a measure of control over their lives and their time. In a sense, such practices must be understood as part of an overarching system that includes shaping schedules, taming professors, and limiting workload.

In the few instances when one can't handle a recalcitrant professor, or has overcommitted time to a paying job, or simply finds course demands to be "busywork" and unfair, then cheating offers an "out"—a way to save time and get the work done without sacrificing one's grade. Students nationwide cheat less as they move up in year, suggesting to me that as they become more skilled in manipulating the other elements of the system, their need to cheat dissipates.

In this light, increases in contemporary rates of cheating reflect not only students' personal ethics but also the shifting societal tides that churn the waters through which students navigate. Political forces, for instance, may determine tuition rates, which decide how many hours a student must work at a job, which affects the amount of time left for coursework, which in turn influences the extent to which cheating becomes a more attractive option.

Cheating, like other aspects of student culture, must be seen as entangled with other issues in the university environment and ultimately with the more telling questions, "What is the purpose of the university?" and "Who gets to go to college?" As we will see in chapter 7, these larger forces affecting university life and hence the student experience must be figured into the equation not just of student cheating but of student culture.

Freshman to Senior: Profile of the Successful Student

In summing up the art of college management, it is instructive to look, finally, at those who have managed well: college seniors. I end this chapter by describing seniors, using national data that compare them with freshmen, as well as insights gleaned from my own research in 2003.

So, what can be said about the successful, savvy senior who has made it most of the way through the public college system?

He or she does not simply get good grades. Rather, the seasoned student has learned to balance, securing good grades, in anticipation of a lucrative and/or satisfying career, while experiencing the joys of college life. More than two-thirds started school with the purpose of pursuing a career that they will enjoy or that will enable them to become financially successful.

The most successful seniors are those who have managed to control the demands of college on their lives. They have learned how to cultivate faculty, choose courses and schedules wisely, negotiate the bureaucracy of college life, and cheat less. Although the details differ from student to student, this upper-

classman's statement captures many features of this transformation process:

> Now I am kind of over the whole "let's have fun all the
> time" idea. This past summer my mom told me I have to
> graduate on time in two more years because she is not pay-
> ing for my tuition after that. Well, this was definitely a
> wake-up call. In order to graduate on time I have to take at
> least six classes a semester from here on out. . . . And don't
> forget about working to eat and pay bills as well. . . .
>
> I think I was pampered the first two years with thinking
> it was great that I am living on my own and taking on
> some responsibilities and experiencing, you know, the
> "fun" of college life. Now I am taking sixteen credits with
> a lab class and it is hard! Now I am experiencing the
> "stress and pressure" of college life. I'm bombarded now
> with responsibilities. The problem I have now is, people
> are frustrating to me because they don't take school seri-
> ously enough.

While "classic" college life, with its fun, alcohol, and sociability, is more prominent in the earlier years, the senior mentality
follows more closely the model of the career-minded "new outsider." Seniors progressively pull out of "college life," and their
hours spent socializing as well as participating in campus activities decrease as the time that they wrest from social and
campus activities is funneled into paid jobs. By the time they
are seniors, 88 percent of students will be working either on or
off campus.

As seniors, they will ask more questions in class, but they
will come to class slightly more often without completing readings or assignments. Despite the escalating sophistication and
relevance of upper-level and major courses, they will not increase the number of study or preparation hours they devote to
them. In response to required courses outside their major, a majority of AnyU upperclassmen will agree that taking the class
has not affected their interest in the subject one way or the

other.[22] If class learning is exciting or self-revelatory, then all the better; but, except where it impacts one's career, learning is incidental.

Most seniors will agree that they've forgotten much of what they learned from classes, even from the semester before. Looking back on college, they will claim to have learned more about themselves, their abilities, and their relationships than about subject areas. And when all is said and done, they will be satisfied with their college experience: 87 percent will rate it "good" or "excellent."[23]

CHAPTER 7

Lessons from My Year as a Freshman

This chapter serves as a response to questions others ask me and questions that, since my freshman year, I keep asking myself. What did I learn personally from this experience? What can undergraduate culture tell us about the larger picture of the American university and its future trajectory?

I begin here with the first question and admit up front that what I learned personally was indeed personal and is still, perhaps, in transition. This is not the only response to what I discovered about undergraduate life, but I thought that the reader might want to see how I am coming to terms, both practically and analytically, with my dual vantage points on academic life. I hold out my conclusions not as advice but rather as food for thought that students and teachers can share.

Students and Teachers: A Cross-cultural Conversation

Entering "the field" (anthropologists' term for the setting in which they do their observations) and leaving the field are special moments, because these transitions often breed significant insights about the place called the field, the place called home, and the relationship between them. In my case, crossing the imaginary line from teacher to student and then back again was accompanied by commentary from both other teachers and other students that is worth reflecting on.

In the last weeks of the spring semester, as I was preparing to attend summer Previews as an incoming freshman, colleagues asked what I would be doing for my sabbatical. I didn't always mention which university, but I told them that I was getting ready to begin fieldwork for an ethnography of undergraduate life, and would be going back to school and living in a dormitory as a freshman. "You're doing WHAT???" was the inevitable response, accompanied by a bimodal reaction—either horrified or tickled. "Are you out of your mind?" one colleague asked me. "You're not seriously intending to move in with eighteen-year-olds?" queried another. The idea of becoming a student in residence was such a stretch for most colleagues that three individuals (two professors and an administrator), in different conversations, responded with the same extraordinary comment that my project sounded just like *Black Like Me,* John Howard Griffin's classic 1960 book about a white man who, by injecting himself with pigment-altering dyes and changing his appearance, lived as a "Negro" in the deep South. Likening my projected freshman experience to changing one's racial identity in the 1950s American South said volumes about the psychological distance educators perceive between their world and that of their students.[1]

I could sense a similar process, in reverse, when I left the field and let it be known that I was leaving school to resume my teaching job, and in the four instances during the year when I had thought it necessary to tell fellow students that I was a professor.[2] Despite my professorial age and demeanor, the reaction was usually one of shock and amazement, followed occasionally by mistrust (was I spying?) but more usually by an appreciation of my willingness to cross over a great divide and "see how it really is as a student."

Perceptions of both difference and hierarchy played a role in these teacher and student reactions, and spoke to the bounded domain we believe the other to inhabit and the mystery and social distance we attribute to that world. Going back and forth between worlds as I did was a bit like extended cross-cultural travel: it was easier to see the incomplete picture each set of natives had about the other's world after finding a "home" in each. Most professors have no idea what a dorm room looks like, or about the routes of the campus bus system, or the cost of books, tuition, and housing. Most students have no understanding of faculty rank, how the university actually functions, or how professors advance in their careers. They have little appreciation for the after-hours work that goes into staging the courses they are taking, and no inkling of what teachers are required to do besides teach.

This kind of ignorance, as international students argued, leads to misperceptions and sometimes intolerance at both ends. Students and faculty encounter each other in distinct and hierarchical roles, and this conditions the way we experience each other. It is easy to see students as irresponsible, deceitful, and self-indulgent, just as it is easy to see teachers as officious, unkind, and self-important.

As I made my transition out of my student role, I tried to hold on to the way in which I had come to know students, even as I donned the mantle of a professor. In the dorms I had developed an affection and respect for students as a class that I had once reserved only for specific individuals. I had observed students managing their identities, placating their parents, positioning their future, and finding their place in peer circles. I can vividly remember overhearing the authentic excitement in one student's voice when she exclaimed into her cell phone, "Mom, the professor told me my essay was really good!" I keep that image of what is at the other end of a professor's encouragement.

I also had my own trials and tribulations as a student. It surprised my colleagues to learn that I was a decent but not a superlative student, and though I did "A" work in a couple of courses, in another I was easily the worst student in the class. Despite my going to AnyU's tutoring center, and wasting too many lost hours on homework problems in that course, the material remained over my head. As I found myself dropping further and further behind, it became a struggle for me to go to class. I came to understand what it means to be on the fence between giving up and making more of an effort. Sometimes nothing more than a teacher's outreach pushes the balance. All these memories now temper the way I interpret new experiences in my professorial role. If there is one lesson that I found most supported by my freshman experience, it is the lesson of compassion.

I also find myself interpreting the undergraduate culture I lived through the eyes of a seasoned academic in order to discover not just its lived realities but its potentials. There are many things I understand about undergraduate culture that, when I reflect beyond my relativist anthropological frame, I don't like. I cannot ignore the observations of international students, or the blindness about racism, or the normalization of cheating.

In the end, it is not just my bounded experiences as teacher and then as student that inform this chapter but rather my ideas of being a teacher after having been a student, and of student life after being a teacher, which I hope to integrate.

Re-entry: The Student as Teacher

It is the summer after my freshman year and I am once again "the teacher." I am preparing for an introduction to anthropology course in the fall semester which I have taught before. I envision walking into the room of ninety students or so—how they sit waiting to meet their new teacher, how the room will grow quieter when I enter, how students who want overrides will recount their reasons for having to get into my class.

I look at my old syllabus, my old notes, my old assignments, thinking how I will update my course. It is not the content that I notice most but the tacit assumptions that are built in to the fabric of the course. My syllabus and other choices grew out of long experience in teaching. I typically teach this class at a popular midday hour on Tuesdays and Thursdays, and follow it or precede it with office hours to encourage visits. I carefully apportion readings, assigning a reasonable number of articles or chapters per week, so that they are manageable and roughly correspond to my lectures. I begin my lectures exactly on time to discourage tardiness, and start new material wherever I ended last time so that there is a logic and continuity to the narrative.

So it always comes as a surprise to me that students appear clueless about what happened in the last class, that only a minority of them have done the reading assigned, and that almost no undergraduates ever show up for my office hours unless perhaps they are failing.

I see now what I didn't see before. In the time between my Tuesday and Thursday classes in introductory anthropology I have taught only one other class, and I have spent at least some time on Wednesday arranging my Thursday class presentation. By contrast, my students have had at least four other classes in between, maybe more, and they have completed many other reading and writing assignments in the interim, in addition, perhaps, to working a job and attending residence hall or club programs.

If they were like me as a student, they feel virtuous that they're present for class, that they remembered to bring the right notebook, and that they managed to catch a bus that has delivered them on time. When class ends at 10:50, they will be off to another bus and another class, because they have designed a schedule, just as I did as a teacher, that apportions blocks of work and free time. While I am there for office hours right after class, they are taking another class with another professor who starts right on time to discourage lateness.

My course, I have come to realize more keenly, is just one of the many balls being juggled in the time management challenge faced by each student. As I realized, and wrote in chapter 6, most mature students will convert the web of demands on their time into some more proactive form of course management. They will figure out what must be done and what can be let go, just as they will decide whether and when to invest more time than I expected. These decisions will be made in the context of a student's own interests and priorities, to be sure, but my own behavior and course structure can appreciably affect how that prioritization works. Take the question of reading for class.

To Read or Not to Read: What the Cultural Experts Say.   I was particularly fascinated by the question of "reading" for class during my year as a student because of my class experiences as a professor, when I found the number of people who seemed not to complete assigned readings in my classes to be both troubling and astounding. Did they just not read the syllabus, I had speculated? I tried repeating the assignment verbally in the class before it was due: "Remember to read article X because I'd like to talk about it next time." Was it too time-consuming to read at the reserve desk at the library, or to copy the articles to read later? I put all the article readings on-line as well as in hard copy for easy access. Yet, despite these efforts, I didn't perceive an appreciable difference in class preparation. Either most of the class hadn't read all the articles or they hadn't read them in a thorough enough way so that we could have a discussion.

But then, as a student, I encountered the same dearth of class preparation. There were frequent pre-class exchanges among fellow students—"Did you do the reading?" or "What was the reading about?"—particularly as the semester went on. Seeing the same behavior across courses and professors, I began to question other students about the considerations that went into their decision whether to do the reading or not. It is a classic anthropological strategy: go to a cultural expert, a native who is particularly skilled and knowledgeable in a subject area, and attempt to reproduce the rules and the considerations that he or she uses to make decisions.

How does a "cultural expert" decide whether or not to read something for class? What are the tacit rules governing his or her decision? After interviewing juniors and seniors about course preparation, and in seeking their advice, I discovered that cultural experts don't casually or lightly discard assignments; rather, they mentally ask themselves a series of questions:

"Will there be a test or quiz on the material?"
"Is the reading something that I will need in order to be able to do the homework?"
"Will we directly discuss this in class in such a way that I am likely to have to personally and publicly respond or otherwise 'perform' in relation to this reading?"

If the answer to all of these questions is *no,* then don't do the reading. At least, I found that the probability of not doing the reading is much higher.

As I became acculturated as a student, I became more finely attuned to the conditions under which class preparation did and did not occur. My personal epiphany came one day several weeks into a mildly interesting lecture course as I was taking notes near the end of the class period. It was well after midterms, and there were final projects, papers, and presentations looming in all my courses. The professor mentioned that he had put an extra article on a Web site that would amplify the subject of his next lecture and that he would like us to read it for the next class. As he began reciting the Web address, I found myself chuckling, realizing that I had no intention of doing this reading and would not even copy down the information. It was immediately clear to me why students had not read articles for my class: there was no strong signal from me that I would use the article—in a quiz or an assignment or even a guaranteed discussion—and, apart from the exceptionally interested student, I had given no reason to prioritize these readings above obligations for other classes.

The answer to the problem of reading that I now favor is to hone the assignments to those I will actually employ in my classes while at the same time creating new classroom forums for making direct and immediate use of the readings I seriously want my students to prepare. I could see why my former "solutions" had not changed their behavior. Like many of my teaching and administrative colleagues, I often design solutions to student problems that do not address the actual source of the problem. The miscalculations come from faulty assumptions concerning what good students do and how they organize their academic lives.

Imperfect Policy.   Just a few examples will suffice to show how assumptions that do not reflect the reality of student life can lead to weak analyses, bad policy, or ineffective solutions to problems.

- When I went to register on-line as an AnyU student, I found that the new computer program that listed course schedules permitted students to search for classes only by course title, subject area (art, business, engineering, and so on), and professor. I could not find out which 9 AM courses were still open. Administrators who put the system into effect obviously didn't think that students should or would search for classes simply by day and time, perhaps because they didn't feel that it was "academically correct" to take a class simply because of its time slot. Thus, we could not see what open classes existed in the university at 2:20 PM on Tuesdays and Thursdays, so crucial because that course would complete our perfect schedule. Students crafting their schedules, including me, were outraged. Once in a while, as any student can tell you, even good students just need a course that fits a particular time slot.

- One of the pieces of information I tried to get about academic life was how often students actually use the library to take out books. The library was able to furnish me with statistics about its excellent inter-library loan service, which allowed students to access articles and books that our library did not own. Although students using inter-library loan often ordered multiple articles or books, it was still the case that in a university of more than thirteen thousand undergraduate students, there were only 1,421 requests for journal articles or book chapters and loans such as monographs, government documents, and microfilm and video materials in the course of an entire academic year. Figuring an average of three requests per patron, this means that only 3 or 4 percent of undergraduates ever requested academic materials, a total that the library professional who furnished me with the data characterized as very low. She believed, though, that it was a problem of communication—that most undergraduates do not realize that they can order items from other libraries and that the service is free. The solution to underuse, then, becomes better advertising.

For me as a former student, that solution doesn't fit the problem. For most papers that an undergraduate will complete, the window of time that the student typically creates to write a paper is a few days, at most a week, and more likely one evening. If a source is not available within this window, it is unlikely that it will be used. That is why I have high hopes for on-line library services as opposed to interlibrary loan arrangements.

- Most professors and administrators overestimate the role that academics plays in student culture, and as a result they magnify the impact of teachers and classes on student life and decisions. For instance, it is widely assumed that more contact time between professors and students will raise student retention rates, and that faculty counsel and advice is an essential part of a student's freshman transition. But at AnyU, when in 2002 a graduate student researcher queried freshmen about their first-year and their reasons for continuing as students, "faculty" was one of the least frequently mentioned reasons. Likewise, in a national survey of more than 30,000 students, researchers found that "students are far more likely to turn to their peers than campus faculty or staff for support during their transition to college. Over 80 percent of students reported interacting with campus friends *daily*, while a significantly smaller percentage of the sample indicated that they interacted with faculty, academic advisors, or other college personnel even on a *monthly* basis."[3]

There is no doubt that special professors do make a difference in the life of specific students, but overall, I'd suggest, student-teacher relationships play a relatively minor role in the experience of undergraduate life in a large university.

In looking beyond the local details of the incidents just recounted, I find that they are illustrative of a point relevant for all universities: the need to tie university services and policy, more directly to student culture. Educational policy, I believe, cannot afford to rely on inaccurate or idealized versions of what students are, and student issues should be analyzed with a fuller understanding of how they are embedded in student culture. From the student networks described in chapter 3, it should be clear that achieving genuine diversity on campus demands a more proactive approach than simply recruiting a more racially diverse student body. Lack of diversity is embedded in the fundamental ways in which students come together, in how they choose their friends and courses, and in the very issue of "choice." Enhancing diversity necessarily entails taking on these larger issues, many of which superficially appear quite removed from the question of diversity itself. The tentacles of the wider society reach deep into university life, making some college practices more deeply rooted than policy can really touch. American consumerism is a good example. Faculty often joke uncomfortably about the number and types of late-model vehicles in the student parking lots as compared with their own. But a sporty car, the latest iPod, frequent dinners out, and a cellphone are just some of the many "must haves" in contemporary college culture that quietly reshape it. Students work jobs not just for their tuition but for a lifestyle to which all have grown accustomed—with the result that there are fewer hours for academics and more need for easy As and homework shortcuts. In addition, students with "stuff" have no use for many community facilities and activities because they have resources of their own. Seen in this light, some new university policy designed to fix "academic underpreparation" or "community participation" can seem hopelessly quixotic.

Reflection: The Teacher as Student

There are parts of student life and student culture that I scrutinize with the more critical eye of a teacher rather than as a "culturally relative" ethnographer. Understanding undergraduate culture—even performing it as a student—doesn't necessarily mean that I categorically support it as a professor.

It is tempting to address the negatives in student culture with a frontal attack, for instance, dealing with drug and alcohol abuse on campus, as one government Web site promotes, by heavily scheduling classes on Fridays: "This strategy emphasizes the importance of academics and discourages the alcohol-fueled partying that may occur on Thursday nights if students do not need to attend classes on Fridays."[4]

Policies and programs like this, in my thinking, position students as errant children who must be thwarted or outwitted. I believe that policy works best when it reflects a positive regard for the judgment of those it seeks to influence and a respect for the resiliency of the culture it wishes to change. While I'm not sure that it is ever productive to "fight" culture, I do believe that one can support what is already present in the culture, albeit in private space or minority opinions. Student culture has this depth and complexity, which often hold the key to its engagement, a point I can illustrate with a particularly poignant memory.

I think of the time when Ray, my study buddy, and I decided to meet at 10 PM in my room to prepare for our French midterm exam the next day. We were both good students in this particular class, and we selected each other as study mates because of our similar academic abilities and common dorm residence. This was not the first time we had studied together, and we joked easily as well as challenged each other, in turn, on the material. I had just finished testing Ray on a series of vocabulary terms when he began questioning me on the past imperfect tense. "Forget that," I responded. "She said it's not on the test." What he said next shocked me. "Is that the only reason you are learning this material . . . for the test? Don't you want to learn to speak French better? Come on, do it."

I was mortified, really, and caught between my two roles. He was right, of course, but not from the standpoint of public student culture, which I had learned to imitate. Because we were friends, he could make that comment to me; but I had long since discovered that in the daily encounters in the dorm and the classroom, there were standard cultural conventions that marked someone as "one of us." What he said to me was nothing one would normally say in public. As a matter of fact, it's the kind of comment that would get one identified as a "witch" in class (see chapter 5).

Like other students wishing to fit in, I responded to the unspoken pressure to make the appropriate critical remark about the class, to emphasize how little I had studied for my decent grade, or to reduce my academic focus to what was on the test. Michael Moffatt noted the same type of discourse in student life a generation ago, a style he called "Undergraduate Cynical." I ended up coming to a very similar conclusion to his when he wrote: "At first I mistook Undergraduate Cynical for a privileged form of truth, for what undergraduates really thought among themselves when all their defenses were down. Eventually I realized that, as a code of discourse, Undergraduate Cynical could be just as mandatory and just as coercive as other forms of discourse."[5]

As observers of American culture have pointed out, this kind of voluntary conformism is an endemic feature of American life that is hardly limited to universities.[6] Despite our celebrated freedom to choose, we seem to choose the same things, and those "free" choices are the badges of our belonging. So it is with student life, in everything from the kind of backpack or the choice of shoes one wears to the kinds of images and words one displays on one's door and the topics one initiates for conversation in the dorm.[7] The conformity is so complete that, in my tallied observations of clothing worn on the walking quad, more than 90 percent of walkers dressed from the same narrow list of items; those who didn't could be singled out in a different social category from the "normal" student—either an overseas student, a member of a marked subgroup such as "goth" or "skater," or a staff member.

It is difficult to evaluate student culture critically when you are aged eighteen to twenty-two, because peer culture is so compelling, but it is not impossible. I met many students like

Ray who privately critiqued one or more aspects of undergraduate culture. I met others, particularly those heavily involved in social, environmental, and ethical issues, who openly rejected many student culture norms and belonged to contesting subcultures.

These alternative "texts" in college life, both within subcultures and operating within the same individual, hold the potential for challenging the more troublesome aspects of undergraduate culture. It is these texts that I have come to enlist when addressing many classroom questions that involve student culture. Thus, I do realize that the "easy A" courses are a necessary part of student scheduling, but the majority of students I met did not *simply* want funny profs and lightweight courses semester after semester. This is why one heard, even sometimes from the same students who touted their easy A, about the argument analysis course they loved that was "not easy but worth it" or the women's studies course they recommended that was "hard but not boring." And although a degree of deceptiveness is endemic in student-teacher relations, the one senior who made perhaps the clearest statement of calculated "working the teacher"—declaring how she purposely wrote a paper contrary to her own belief in order to flatter the professor's political stance—identified the same course as the one in which she'd learned the most of all her college courses. I take such examples to mean that the actual experience of individual students is much richer than the normative expressions of student culture.

When I contest certain aspects of undergraduate culture—by refusing to "dumb down" a course, say, and make it an "easy A"—I feel that I am aligning myself with students, and the internal dialogues of students, that already exist in undergraduate culture. Similarly, in forewarning my students that I will seriously pursue instances of cheating on exams, I do so with the understanding and specific acknowledgment that the great majority of students don't cheat the great majority of the time. In enforcing such policies, I feel that I am protecting my students, not persecuting them, and making sure that the ninety-five out of one hundred of my students who have taken the time to read and study for a test are not betrayed by my lack of vigilance. I exclude behaviors such as doing homework together or discussing paper topics as "cheating," because fighting the natural reciprocity of student life seems an unwarranted and, to me, disagreeable battle.

After completing this project, and writing this book, I see more clearly in hindsight that my journey into student life was, in a certain sense, a way of combating my own alienation as a professor. Such alienation is a common malaise of my time and profession. It is, in part, generational, when I see how my students distance themselves from the hard-fought earlier battles for civil rights and gender equality; it is, in part, a result of the culture war, as I've watched student assaults across the country on academics critical of U.S. foreign policy or the war in Iraq in the wake of 9/11;[8] it is, in part, institutional, as the control of the university's mission and direction slips increasingly from faculty hands.

But in addressing the aspects of my alienation that concerned students, my quest was largely successful for me. I wish that more teachers could see students and student culture from "the other side." They would be privy to more of the hopes and trials, dreams and tribulations, bravery and kindness that call on our common humanity. Teachers would come to know that when a student openly snoozes in class, or invents a story about why the paper hasn't been written on time, or wants an override into a course because of its time slot, this is the small stuff, the workings of a culture. As hard as it may be to realize sometimes, it is really not personal.

As for students, I wish they could more readily see that classroom bureaucracy arises from the recurrent behavior of the thousands of students who have gone before them; that their silence in class can make an enthusiastic professor lose his energy and a new teacher doubt her abilities; or that finding a student cheating is not a triumphant moment, as one student suggested to me, but an upsetting one. Teachers, after all, are human too, but perhaps it will take a student-turned-teacher to credibly tell those tales.

Student Culture and "Liminality"

The personal experiences, both my own and others', described in this book are instances of student culture. They may seem far removed from abstract questions about the nature of the university, its trajectory, and the wider culture. In truth, though, there is a profound connection between them—between what goes on in students' lives, the direction in which our universities are headed, and even the unfolding of our larger culture. To explore this connection, please allow me a little anthropology.

When Moffatt titled his ethnography of college life *Coming of Age in New Jersey,* he was alluding to the notion of college as a rite of passage.[9] In anthropological parlance, these are the rituals that shepherd individuals and groups from one stage in the life cycle to another. As they do this from one generation to the next, such rites become part of the intimate biographies of a society's members as well as part of the way the society reproduces and regenerates itself. College can be considered such a rite of passage.

Cross-culturally, rites of passage have universal characteristics marked by severance from one's normal status, entrance into a "liminal" state where normal rules of society are lifted, and finally reintegration into society within a new status.[10] This jibes well with the nature of the undergraduate college experience: eighteen-year-olds leave the strictures and comforts of their parents' home; they enter a geographically removed youth-based college culture with its own rules and values; then, as I found, as their senior year approaches, students increasingly turn their attention to "life after school," only to be welcomed instantly as new alumni and stalwarts of the larger society at the moment of graduation.

It is in the middle or "liminal" state—the ambiguous place of being neither here nor there—that anthropologists see profoundly creative and transformative possibilities. "Liminal" states throughout the world, as the anthropologist Victor Turner has pointed out, lift the normal constraints on behavior and bring participants into new relationships with one another. In the U.S. college, as universally, liminal people who might otherwise have differential status in the society become equals, and those who share the ritual experience of lowliness, homogeneity, and comradeship establish strong emotional, almost sacred bonds.[11] Undergraduate culture itself becomes this liminal communal space where students bond with one another, sometimes for life, and, amid rules of suspended normality and often hardship, explore their identities, wrestle with their parents' world, and wonder about their future.

Liminal experiences, Turner argues, contain the seeds of enormous creativity and, indeed, of wider social change. By way of the ritual process, because here people slip through the cracks of normal cultural classifications and roles, they get the chance to catch glimpses of themselves when not embedded in structure, unleashing uncanny new visions. They ideally share, too, in the creation of new egalitarian relations between people normally separated by status differentiations such as social class, gender, ethnicity, age, sexual orientation, or religion. In this way, experiences of liminality may help to liberate "the human capacities of cognition, affect, volition, creativity" and thereby prompt innovative responses to the social system, and to the feelings of alienation, exploitation, and divisiveness that it may spawn.[12]

Such possibilities represent the promise of the university. Like all rites of passage, college is at once an affirmation and preparation for the world *and* a creative response and innovative challenge to that same world. A society and the institutional rites of passage within it should not, in cross-cultural perspective, be replicas of each other; they exist instead in a dialectical relationship in which they can shape and influence each other. For the university, this means that, just as the society will affect the future of our universities, what happens in student culture—or what doesn't happen—helps forge the shape of our society.

Will the liminal life of college culture allow students to arrive at inspired new ideas for society and transformative visions of our world? Or will it simply train young people to become adults who take their place in line in the workforce of the existing society? Can it do both? And how will we know when college culture is tilted too far in one direction or the other? It is through this perspective and these questions that I invite you to consider what you have read so far and the connections described in the next section among student culture, the university's mission, and the larger American culture.

Student Culture, the Public University, and American Culture

Being a student completed a sort of university cycle for me, providing a view of the same university from the last of its major vantage points. A faculty member for many years, I have seen the university as a graduate and as an undergraduate teacher who served for multiple terms on our faculty senate. I have also spent a recent administrative year as a "faculty fellow" in AnyU's Office of the President, which gave me special access to planning and policy meetings in the university and the state. After seeing student culture up close and making my faculty-administrative-student circle complete, I find that one thing is very clear to me. The trajectories of the university and of student culture are intimately entwined, and the reason why they are intertwined is that the same forces shaping the university are shaping student culture.

Since World War II and the GI bill, the United States has had an explosive increase in the number and proportion of Americans who go to college. While 16 percent of the population attended college in 1940, by 1961, 48 percent of those who finished high school went on to college; by 1981, it was 53.9 percent; and by 2001, it was 61.7 percent.[13] Beginning in the Reagan administration, federal funding of this educational democratization began to decline proportionally; state governments, with new "downloaded" federal mandates, found education budgets competing, often unfavorably, with pressing needs of health care, welfare, and prisons. Between 1985 and 1995, states across the country slashed their direct appropriations to universities by almost 25 percent.[14] By 2000, total government revenue accounted for only half of the public university budget.[15] This situation has only worsened in the post-9/11 era, and these financial facts have been the single most important driving force in university planning for more than a decade. How does a university find ways to support itself?

Most of the issues discussed at the highest levels of the university somehow involve this question, because public colleges and universities are scrambling for "revenue streams" to make up their budget shortfalls and for new ways to recapture public monies. For educational institutions across the country, this has meant implementing a series of strategies to stay financially afloat. Among the most important have been the push to cultivate a closer relationship to corporate and business interests, an increased reliance on tuition for funding (and on attracting full-tuition-paying students to the university), and more pragmatic appeals to state legislatures encouraging curriculum and research initiatives that contribute directly to the economic development of the state.

These agendas are reflected clearly in where the money goes within the contemporary university. Funding nationwide for libraries and instruction has dropped steadily since 1985 (despite a college population that increasingly requires remedial instruction).[16] At the same time, the percentage of university budgets allocated to "administration" has climbed.[17] New and expanded administrative roles have been created to lobby the legislature, fundraise from alumni and court personal and corporate donors, and market degree and certificate programs to (paying) students.

Universities now look to corporations not just for donations but also for university-corporate partnerships in degree programs, in student housing, and in patents and research that are expected to defray costs or contribute revenues to the university's bottom line.[18] Many university entities—such as bookstores and campus eateries—have been privatized or have been pressed into becoming self-supporting, and increasingly, entire curricular units, such as distance education programs, are expected to do the same. To pay for programs and replace retired faculty, professors must now make funding pleas based on the department's "student credit hour production" and its likelihood of attracting new students, as determined by marketing tools such as surveys of student interest. The "star faculty" at universities are its entrepreneurial grant and patent getters who bring revenue into the university. Indeed, as universities run on the same principles as businesses, they come to resemble them.[19]

One of the most consistent strategies for making up funding shortfalls has been tuition increases. Between 1991–92 and 2001–2, tuition at public colleges rose by 21 percent and at private colleges by 26 percent, and this is *after* adjustment for inflation is figured in.[20] More and more, students (and their families) are being asked to make up for the difference between what the government allocates to public universities and the actual cost of running them.

At the same time, students constitute an increasingly less elite economic segment of society, which means that the average student is poorer than those in the past. And although scholarships and grants have increased with tuition hikes, the raises have not been proportional. A 2004 government report found that increases in tuition and fees during the preceding decade had outpaced both inflation and growth of the median family income.[21] The result has been debt—a huge amount of debt that college students are incurring for the sake of their education—and a sharp rise in the percentage of borrowers among full-time undergraduates.[22] It is no wonder that students are increasingly attracted to majors with clearly associated job titles, that most students need to work while going to school, and that undergraduates' priorities include getting good grades and positioning themselves for the labor force through internships and targeted volunteerism.

It is easy to see how some aspects of contemporary student culture were formed. To reduce running debt even higher, most students must now work and go to school at the same time, which has the added corollary of compressing their academic activities into ever smaller time slots. To repay their debts, students are anticipating the need for immediate and lucrative employment after college, so they choose both "practical" and "well-paying" fields of study, resulting in the decline of majors such as philosophy, history, and English literature. The majors for which there have been the largest proportional increases in degrees conferred since 1980 include business, computer science, parks and recreation, protective services, and the health professions.[23] These degree choices, in turn, funnel new budgetary allocations to these same departments and programs, one of many feedback processes that close the loop between the paths of students and the direction of universities.

Together, the exigencies of students and of universities are resulting in a more market-driven and market-focused university. There are positive aspects to this development. Universities today are probably more responsive to students' needs for easy registration, comfortable housing, and a seamless transfer of credits. To attract paying students, they are more accommodating of a wider variety of student constraints, such as where and when one can attend classes, which has enabled more nontraditional students to enroll.

The career focus in higher education has its upside as well. Cursing the ties between college, jobs, and upward mobility is a privilege of the elite. As a professor, I am heartened by the idea that a degree can serve as a vehicle for economic mobility, especially as college has become an option for an ever wider economic segment of the U.S. public. In this way the public college and university become a force not only for mobility but also for equity in our society. Similarly, it is hard to rail against the university's stepping down from its ivory tower to serve the social and economic needs of the state, so long as the state doesn't become the tail that wags the dog.

But there are important warning signs as well on the road universities are traveling. The market-driven university is likely to experience the same pitfalls as businesses and market-places. Businesses do not gear themselves toward those without money. When student aid is not commensurate with tuition increases, competition for scholarship money intensifies, and many applicants are cast by the wayside. We are already seeing poorer students retreating to community colleges, leaving the public four-year university less diverse than it would otherwise be.[24] Degree programs tightly geared to the marketplace become products themselves, and are likely to bust and boom with the fickleness of the times. A university held to market principles will try, just as a business does, to produce more for less, particularly in times of declining revenues. This is why students are seeing larger classes as well as a growing cadre of cheaper part-time and non–tenure track teachers in the classroom. Although these instructors are often the most committed and talented educators, they are also the ones most likely to be overworked, to be grossly underpaid, and to have the least voice in the curricular and governance decisions at their universities.

Students, their parents, and teachers ought to keep a close watch on these changes in the university, because they—we—are ultimately the guardians of the university's very special functions in society. There are serious questions about how universities can maintain their "liminal" transformative qualities when the world is so much with them. Although we may want universities to address the needs of our states and our businesses, we cannot rely on either the politics of government or the profits of corporations to guide the educational mission. In the long run, we would not want a university to become so immersed in the world as it is that it can neither critique that world nor proffer an ideal vision of how else it might be. These are purposes of universities that none of us should surrender.

A Final Reflection

I end this book, true to ethnographic form, with a description of an event—one that I hope will spur thought and discussion among students and teachers. The event is not particularly emotional or dramatic, but I have thought about it many times, both as a student and as a teacher.

There are actually two events involved, and the questions lie between them. These were, significantly, the only mandatory freshman events beside our president's convocation, and both were part of the Welcome Week introduction to our "living and learning" university community. One was the book discussion group, previously mentioned, where we began our academic investigation as students into "the educated person." The other was a presentation on "making college count" that was billed more seductively as "Unleashing Your Inner Monster."

I have seen the presentation twice now. Apparently universities and colleges all over the country arrange this same program for incoming freshmen because it is lauded by students and free to universities. The speakers are employed and trained by a nonprofit division of a for-profit company (originally an ad agency) which "services the labor recruitment needs of 130,000 employers world-wide," according to its Web site. AnyU freshmen were asked to attend one of a few identical scheduled hour-long presentations. There were no faculty present, because the event was staged before classes began, and the large auditorium, which filled with freshmen, quickly became an all-student space.

As the session begins, a good-looking, dynamic young woman (or in some sessions a man) strides out onto the stage with a high-tech microphone wrapped around her head, like a Big Ten football coach. Using a language, humor, and style that is familiar and appealing, the presenter says she knows what we're thinking: "When is the first big party?" "How much do I really have to study?" "Will I make it here?"

The speaker identifies with her audience: "You're starting college. I recently graduated. Let me tell you what you need to know to make this experience worth it." So, "Why are you here?" she asks, naming several possibilities. A number of hands go up when she suggests "to get out of the house," a very few raise their hands for "to learn more," and more than half the hands shoot up for "to get a job." "All right," the speaker says, anticipating this response, so let's look at what you can do now in college to make that happen."

"Employers expect to hire 36 percent fewer college graduates than they did one year ago," we are told. "How can you set yourself apart?" A number of entertaining vignettes follow. Using volunteers from the audience, and play-along pages from a color booklet we've all been given, the speaker shows us how what we do right now in college will ultimately affect our working lives: how goofing off for just your freshman year can ruin your cumulative average; how not getting involved in student organizations will look on your record later.

In one segment we are asked by the presenter to decide "which person would you hire?" as freshman volunteers play the parts of recent graduates, reading scripts from index cards. One "graduate" tells us that, during college, he joined Habitat for Humanity and helped build houses by pounding nails. The other relates that she became an officer of the same organization, and increased the number of volunteers by 50 percent, which allowed the group to increase the number of houses built. It's clear which one we are meant to prefer. The message to us is to make a recordable impact, even at jobs we don't like, because the people in charge, as the presenter reminds us, can still write letters of recommendation. Keep in mind, we are told, college is a great place to "test drive your career," so make the most of jobs and internships.

The booklets we have been given are peppered with advertisements and with the logos and names of corporate sponsors representing dandruff shampoo, deodorant, a designer clothing label, breath mints, cell phone service, mobile phones and computer games, and a financial firm. When the presentation ends, we exit to upbeat music, each of us carrying a big bag stuffed with company giveaways—candy, cups, pens, free samples, and ads.

I didn't realize at the time how similar the messages embedded in the presentation were to those I would come to recognize widely in student culture. There was the "fun-party-independence-youth" veneer, which is long-standing in student culture, but the more dominant statement of the presentation was one of pragmatism and careerism. Hard work, forethought, and organization were part of this career message to students, but so too was the idea that grades have primacy, that you should join groups with résumé building in mind, that a smart student should "figure out your profs" (the title of one presentation segment), that students are in individual competition with one another for grades and recommendations, and that, above all, college is about positioning yourself for a good job and an affluent future. This was, in short, a fair summary of the cultural model of the "new outsider" identified by Helen Horowitz (see chapter 6), and touched on many of themes I observed in college life, from individualism and instrumental student-teacher relations to résumé-targeted volunteerism and materialism.

Most students leaving the auditorium were audibly animated and seemed to think the presentation was terrific. I had no doubt that it struck a much more resonant chord than the other required activity that we attended less than twenty-four hours later: the book discussion groups that kicked off the Freshman Colloquium course. We went from the young corporate presenter who handed out advice and gifts to professors who led us through a discussion about a novel, set in the nineteenth century, about scientific exploration and the environment.[25] The themes of the discussion groups, which had been orchestrated in advance, centered on citizenship, diversity, the environment, the role of technology. In my freshman seminar that was to follow, we would read about "preparing citizens of the twenty-first century" and consider the central question, "What does it mean to be an educated person?" Yet instead of the career skills and money-focused benefits touted by our opening presentation, the class and the readings would lead us to ideas about the importance of humility, tolerance, self-criticism, the wise use of power, and other attributes of William Cronon's liberally educated person.[26]

It was hard to resist comparing the messages and noting that the themes of our discussion group and the themes of our "getting the most from college" presentation had almost nothing in common, and in some ways could seem diametrically opposed, as when the presenter encourages self-promotion and the professor humility. Welcome Week, like college life, was replete with competing messages about what college was. How are these to be reconciled? Is one message preferable to the other? Can we really have both? Do they put limits on each other?

I think, too, of a recurrent conversation I had as a student. We might be talking about the tribulations of a course, or the hoops students must jump through to get a degree, and then someone will say that he can't even remember what he learned just a semester before. Someone else will say, "Yeah, it's all bogus because you'll forget 99 percent of the specifics in all those classes anyhow." So what's the point? If one *does* forget the details of information from a semester ago, and if the technical material you learn in your major will likely be obsolete in five years, and if you will probably change careers several times in your lifetime anyhow, then what is worth learning?

In the end, the paths taken by higher education may be out of all our hands, but understanding our stake in these messages, as students and teachers, and making those stakes known, is our only chance of affecting the way the story of the modern university will unfold.

Afterword
Ethics and Ethnography

This afterword actually tells a story that didn't come to me until my research and my writing were complete, so perhaps it is best read "after the fact." It is a story about research ethics, about the process a researcher goes through beyond the formal rules of research. It is also about the long reach of ethical issues, and how questions of disclosure come to entail a host of unanticipated decisions about what are legitimate data, and even how to write. The story begins, though, *before* the fact—when it first became clear to me that I would actually become a student at my own university and write about my experiences.

Before the Fact

I realized that there were potential ethical dangers in my approach, and so I did what I could to mitigate these before starting the research. There are issues of honesty and trust that must underlie any (research) relationship, and I wrestled with how I could honor these qualities without fully disclosing my identity.

As I contemplated my transformation into a student-who-is-also-a-researcher, the main issues seemed fairly apparent.

There was never any doubt that, in order to interview people or directly record anyone's words, it would be necessary to identify myself as a researcher, explain my study, and obtain written permission to interview and use the interviewee's words in publication. This is basic ethical protocol (i.e., informed consent), and this is, of course, what I did. Whenever soliciting participation in interviews, I explained that I was a researcher, that I was doing a study of undergraduate culture, that my research was *not* for a class or independent study (my addition), and that I intended to publish the results. The Institutional Research Board (IRB) at my university and I concurred that it was not necessary to identify my job (from which I was on sabbatical) as that of a professor at AnyU.

It was not necessary, that is, unless people asked, I had decided. One commitment I made was not actively to lie or otherwise fabricate the details of my life. "Tell if they ask" and "Don't invent an autobiography." These were my own rules, beyond the scope of the IRB agreement, which proceeded from my personal understanding of the basic level of rapport and trust that must accompany anthropological research. If pressed about what else I do, I would say that I was, "among other things," a writer (which is true), and that writing about college life was one of the reasons why I was living in the dorms. If doubly pressed, I would say that I was a professor. This happened only once—and the questioner was a journalism student and friend whose shower of personal queries seemed to warrant a more complete answer than I at first had given. I asked her to keep my confidence, and she did. Most people, though, just weren't that interested.

Being an experienced researcher, I also understood that I needed to take whatever steps I could in advance to protect the source of any information that might be revealed. I anticipated that, as a student, I'd be likely to witness or hear about a number of activities that are either illegal or against university policy—everything from keeping pets in the dorm, to affirmative action violations, to cheating, drinking, and using drugs. Although I intended to act, as any student would, to try to give good advice when asked, and to avert impending disasters that crossed my personal path, I did not want to be or behave in any official role as a representative of the university; neither did I want my work to be viewed as public property which could be solicited by the administration for investigative, policy, or planning purposes.

I consequently gave formal notice to the university that I would "relinquish my role as an officer of the university" (apparently faculty *are* such officers) and submitted advance letters to the offices of both academic affairs and affirmative action, indicating that I would neither record names nor report any violation of university policy or public law.

I also made the express decision to pay for my tuition, room and board, course fees, and books out of pocket rather than apply for internal or external funding, because I was uncertain what rights funding agencies might then have in my field notes or data. It was the most expensive year of fieldwork I have ever undertaken.

The Process of Fieldwork

It seemed to me that I had covered all the ethical bases. It wasn't until my research was no longer an abstraction that other issues came to light. Once we are living and working with people, and immersed in day-to-day interactions, the sensibilities that guide us in our lives (as opposed to the rules that apply in our statements of professional ethics)[1] come to bear. In real life, we make friends. We share confidences. We can see and feel the texture of lived situations and relationships. I let these particulars change my rules somewhat.

In most circumstances and for most relationships I encountered, it was quite comfortable and easy for me to withhold the facts of my non-student life. Few people actively asked me for personal information, and I felt no moral or social pressure to volunteer details about my life that would likely jeopardize my research. It did not seem to be dissimilar from earlier fieldwork decisions to make no mention of my Jewish heritage, for instance, in an overseas Christian community that was largely anti-Semitic. But over time, I found that my "don't ask, don't tell" policy took me only so far.

Several instances arose in which the simple act of withholding information about myself threatened to harm, or at least disturb, other people who had a relationship to me. In three of those instances I ended up disclosing my identity. In each I sensed myself crossing a line of comfort in my secrecy because of the intimacy of real relationships and the responsibility that such closeness entails.

In the first (and earliest) instance, a study mate and student with whom I had become fairly close was applying for an academic scholarship opportunity. (It happened to be the student I call Ray in my final chapter, who admonished me to study in order to learn rather than for the purpose of taking a test.) We studied together regularly for a class we shared that had frequent exams. One night, after a study session, Ray talked with me about an application he was writing that required supporting reference letters from three faculty members.

Ray had told me that he couldn't think of a third faculty member to be a character reference for his application. None of the faculty on his remaining list knew him well, he confided, and he asked me whether I thought he should just ask a teacher who'd given him an A in a big lecture class but probably didn't really know who he was. "I don't think he'll give you a strong and personal enough letter," I told him honestly. In my heart, I knew that the right faculty "character reference" was *me,* sitting silently next to him. I said nothing at the time but after mulling it over, a few days later, after a late night study session, I let Ray know I had something surprising to tell him. It wasn't easy to explain to a disbelieving Ray (at first he thought I was joking with him) that I was really a faculty member. If he wanted, I continued, I would be happy to write a letter of support for him based on my knowledge of his academic habits and commitments. As it turned out, I did end up providing Ray's third reference.

The second case involved my Sexuality class, the course I described in chapter 5. As a condition of group membership, our small, intimate discussion groups were bound by a strict confidentiality agreement about not revealing to others the information or stories that individuals divulged during our semester together. Several weeks into the course, I found that I was relaxed about my role in my discussion group, aware that I would never take notes about these small-group sessions, and committed to continue sharing accurate and personal information about myself with the group.

One particular week more than halfway into the semester, we were given the assignment of interviewing one another about a series of intimate sexual issues and beliefs in our lives. The people I interviewed were very forthcoming about their personal histories and attitudes, as was I, and we completed the assignment. I, of course, had no intention of using any of this material for my book. Yet I began to feel that if my fellow students learned later that I was a professor writing a book, it could trigger alarm and betrayal. I therefore "came out" to the members of my small group, explaining that our class agreement of confidentiality would remain rock solid, and that nothing about their lives or the details of our discussions would ever appear in my book. The fact that I had shared very personal information about my own life eased the situation, and the others reciprocally assured me that they would not be sharing the details of my sexual life with my future students!

A third "coming out" scenario involved my resident assistant (RA), the upperclassman titularly in charge of the corridor on which I lived. In my second semester, as I explain in chapter 1, I dropped some courses to allow me time to conduct my formal project interviews. The RA became concerned that I might be having academic problems and approached me with an offer of help and advice. Was I having trouble keeping up with my classes? Was there anything she could do? I felt that I had to let her know that she needn't worry, and that I was not sinking into an academic hole from which I would never emerge. Her genuine concern triggered a new level of concern in me for my lack of disclosure. I took her aside and told her that, while I'd give her the full story at the end of the year, she ought to know that my situation was not what it appeared. I was a person with advanced degrees, who had come back to school for reasons to do with my writing interests.

In addition to disclosure issues, new questions and finer distinctions emerged, as I conducted my research, about what constituted legitimate data. My research data took many forms. There were formal interviews, accompanied by signed consent documents, and several observations of public spaces (such as cafeterias) and of public discourse (such as graffiti). These seemed relatively unproblematic. But then there were my own daily field notes, which chronicled my personal experiences as a student in my dorm and in my classes. I wrote down everything, from my conversations in the study lounge, to the pre- and post-class conversations I heard in the classroom, to the content of personal exchanges that occurred in the course of a group project of which I was a member.

I overheard many dialogues through the thin walls of my dorm room. Almost every night, in fact, I went to sleep to chatter and laughter from the adjacent rooms and was privy to informative waves of gossip and drama that seeped through my walls. While I learned plenty from these conversations, as I did from many of my lived freshman experiences, it was clear to me that I should not take notes or otherwise record what I heard. That was unambiguously eavesdropping. But what about public conversations in the halls? In my classes? In my study groups? Couldn't I write down what I could legitimately hear or see simply by being present in my dorm or class? Or record my own experiences in a personal journal? But, then again, is it fair to say I can record *anything* I experience as a participant-observer? Can I record my own experiences in a journal if some of those experiences involve other people's words and stories? Was information shared with me done so on the assumption that I was a student, and only a student?

The questions regarding my data seemed to grow more numerous as time and my relationships as a student went on; instead of becoming clearer, the answers to these questions felt increasingly arbitrary. I realized that my level of comfort and certainty was shifting with the depth and quality of my relationships and with the lived concreteness of seeing the data in their human context, that is, as incidents, stories, and conversations attached to real people and real encounters. I did not come to any further resolution of my questions until the writing process began. It was then that push came to shove, so to speak, and choices had to be made.

The Act of Writing

As I wrote, I tried to keep in mind the students with whom I'd gone to school. Some friends, some acquaintances, some just passing faces in my classes—but faces I still recognized on campus. Would I be comfortable saying what I was writing that moment, in that chapter, if I were saying it to them? I tried projecting, too: Would I be comfortable if I were a student and I recognized in a book (written by a professor at my own university) an informal conversation I thought I was having privately with a classmate? These simple considerations radically changed *how* I wrote. I did not approach my writing with rules in mind, but in the act of sitting, composing, and visualizing my "student acquaintance" audience, I found that my writing shifted, and "rules" of a sort emerged.

I remember coming to the section on cheating in chapter 6, actually one of the first chapters that I wrote. I had had some fascinating and spontaneous conversations with students, as a fellow student, about both the idea of cheating and personal incidents of cheating. I did not introduce these topics. They simply came up in the course of being a student, and I recorded the conversations I had, albeit without mentioning names, in my daily field notes. Outlining my chapter on academic life (chapter 5), I saw the way these students' words and stories would bolster and complement the points I wished to make. But relating the details of these stories or directly quoting from student conversations began to feel uncomfortable as I looked with my mind's eye at the people who had shared them with me. I had obtained knowledge of these incidents through personal relationships with other students, and these personal relationships were in part based on their belief that I was a fellow student. It became clear that I couldn't repeat their stories or precise words.

This happened many times, and involved a plethora of topics, and not just those—like cheating—that were "edgy." For instance, I had the privileged ethnographic "participant" position of being a working member of several task groups within classes that were charged with graded activities such as putting on a presentation, making a tape, doing a research project, and so on. These groups, which met outside of class time, were wonderful learning experiences for me. I was privy to private critiques of our class, lessons in how group assignments really work, discussions of social life and campus issues, and more. But when these data entered into the writing process, I felt as if I were literally telling tales out of school. The material was not controversial, but it was based, again, on the default assumption that our interactions were taking place among friends, peers, and nothing more. Despite a rich experiential life as a freshman, I found myself consciously and significantly narrowing the field of information and experience from which I was willing to draw for my book.

As a result, I have in my notes and my memory much richer and more intimate knowledge than I sometimes share directly in this book. Although this knowledge informed my writing, it does not always appear as I encountered it. Knowing, in hindsight, this relationship of text to awareness allows me to give readers a fuller sense of what they are seeing—the principles, if you will, that guided the production of this text.

In general, I can say that the way information was presented was related to the way it was solicited. For reasons of both logistics and propriety, there were some limited times during my fieldwork when I solicited information as a researcher *and* a professor. For instance, in seeking participants for international student interviews, I sent a bulk E-mail notice through the auspices of the international student office. It was one thing for students to assume that I was a student because I was in their class behaving like a student; it was quite another to present myself via E-mail as a student to people I did not know. The idea of writing to a group of students and saying that I was a student doing research seemed a violation of my commitment not to lie directly. So I didn't, which meant that international students spoke with me knowing that I was a professor. For that reason, I felt empowered to use their words verbatim. Chapter 4, about international students, therefore relies heavily on opinions expressed by students, in their own words and in stories or incidents they related. Readers will also notice a greater use of direct quotation when the source of my data was focus groups, which I solicited through a similar public process.

I felt much less comfortable using personal stories or narratives shared with me when the presumption was that I was a student. Although I took greater license with those whom I formally interviewed and from whom I had signed consent forms, even these interviews proceeded on the default assumption that I was a student. As a result, the text may have some unusual features for an ethnography.

I often privileged public information over private information so that, for instance, my discussion of cheating (chapter 6) is presented less through students' personal stories than through their anonymous graffiti, public Web sites, and national studies. Similarly, I was much more likely to repeat a comment made aloud in class and other public utterances than I was to relate a similar remark spoken privately. In general, then, I relied more heavily in my text on incidents and comments in the public domain than I would otherwise do.

Readers may also have noticed my decisions to aggregate data, with the intent of masking personal comments, and to "translate" scenes, either by paraphrasing conversations or by modifying my descriptions to minimize their voyeurism. This meant, for instance, that I occasionally substituted my "participant's-eye view" of my Sexuality class for student dialogue or my own cheating behavior for that of classmates because of the delicate subject matter and the consequent need for privacy. It meant, too, that I regularly walk the reader by the hand through my own perceptions of situations, sharing what I heard and saw rather than what other people said and did. There is occasionally only a fine line between the two approaches, but these choices became my way of addressing the problem of appropriating other students' conversations and lives for my book.

In the end, you can never be sure. I cannot be certain that my internal sense of appropriateness and trust will satisfy every person whose words and stories I used, or all who might imagine that I used their words and stories. I cannot be sure that students reading a book about a university, a class, or a conversation they might recognize, would not feel betrayed.

The semester after I finished my research, I was walking out of a building as a classmate from my freshman seminar was walking in. We had been members of a task group that produced a successful final project, and so we knew each other better than one would know most classmates. We exchanged warm "how you doin'?" small talk. Then my friend asked where I was headed.

"To class," I answered.

"What is it?" she asked.

"Oh, an anthropology class . . . actually I'm teaching it."

"No kidding!" she exclaimed. "How did you get to do that? I want to take it!"

"Well," I answered sheepishly, "it's 'cause I'm actually a professor too. I was a student last year to do some research, but now I'm back to being a professor."

"I can't believe that," she responded and then paused. "I feel fooled."

We have talked since that time about what I did and why I did it, and I believe that her initial feelings have evolved. But still, that was her initial reaction, and it moved me; I imagine that there are a few other fellow students who might feel the same way and with whom I will never have the opportunity to speak.

My insurance in these inevitable cases of unanticipated student reactions, on the one hand, and misjudgments in my writing decisions, on the other, was to make not only the university but myself as well as anonymous as I could. As in most anthropological work, one's "village"—or university, in this case—is designated with a pseudonym, but this ethnography has some interesting twists. To use my real name would be automatically to identify my university and thus, by inference, the field of people whom I am writing about. Under the circumstances, a pen name coupled with a generic university name seemed a reasonable offering to the gods of propriety.

I certainly would have preferred to put my real name on my work, and I am not terribly worried about the possibility that, in time, that information will come to light. But for now, while student friends are still in school, while dorm mates may recognize what they wrote on graffiti boards or the quips on their dorm doors, while classmates may spot familiar conversations, this affords another level of both ambiguity and privacy. A book about a university with an alias, written by an academic author with a pseudonym—however strange that may appear—seemed the best way to go.

Rebekah Nathan, AnyU, October 2004

Notes

1. Welcome to "AnyU"

1. Segal 2000, A64.
2. Rojstaczer 2001.
3. Horowitz 1987, Holland and Eisenhart 1990.
4. Indeed, some important work on these subjects is available in addition to sources already mentioned. See Adler and Adler 1991 on athletics, Sanday 1990 on fraternities, and Bell and McGrane 1999, chap. 13, on student-parent relations.
5. Even Moffatt, whose work is closest to mine, did not attend classes. After attending a week-long orientation where he posed as a student, Moffatt then identified himself as a professor and lived one night per week in the dorm as a professor over a period of two different academic years. The great majority of his data was thus solicited within a professor-student relationship, as has been true for other works that relied on student observations and interviews.
6. I did not live in a freshman dormitory because my presence there would have been too much of an exception—older first-year students were not placed with freshmen—and so I chose a dormitory for upperclassmen, whose residents were primarily, though not exclusively, sophomores and juniors.
7. I ended up listing my high school on the main form along with an asterisk, followed by "please see attached sheet." On the attached sheet I wrote: "For purposes of this application I wish to use my high school transcripts only, but I also attended three other universities, whose credits I do not wish to use. Please contact me if further information is required."
8. "Returning" is a label applied to students who likely attended high school years ago and are coming back to school to continue their educa-

tion. It is a euphemism for "old" rather than a reference to someone who is returning to the university after an absence.

9. For more on college slang and its role in constituting social identity, see Eble 1996.

10. U.S. Department of Education 2002, table 214.

11. I am consciously not attending to a couple of the major trends in higher education, namely, distance education and part-time commuter students with full-time jobs.

2. Life in the Dorms

1. In a given year there are probably almost double this amount. Some boards, however—such as birthday boards—appear each month; others are recycled, moved from one floor to another. I counted these only once.

2. Moffatt 1989, 33.

3. It is important to understand that the connection between culture and individual behavior is not always a direct one. As in the larger world, so it is in the dorms. The frequent images of and references to drinking, for instance, are both real and symbolic. Students certainly drink, but most reserve drinking for appropriate times, even though its imagery is everywhere. In interviews it was commonplace to hear upperclassmen explain that they're not "into the bar and drinking scene" or how they've learned to moderate their drinking, unlike freshmen, who are still young and foolish.

4. See, for instance, Rubington 1990.

5. I conducted one-hour interviews with fourteen hall mates, ten of whom completed time diaries of their activities for a two-day period during selected weeks. In all, I sampled twenty days of diary information—a small sample, but one in which I knew the people, and thus the context of the information I was receiving.

6. Moffatt 1989, 32–33.

7. National Survey of Student Engagement (NSSE) 2003.

8. Not all "downtime" was included. I excluded eating alone and running errands either alone or with others but included napping and telephone and Internet exchanges with friends as relaxing or socializing.

9. Moffatt (1989) reported that approximately one-quarter of students spent one to two hours a day in extracurricular activities. The NSSE 2003 survey found that 42 percent of seniors and 36 percent of freshmen didn't participate in any "co-curricular" activities, and 31 percent of students participated only one to five hours in an entire week.

10. In my small sample, students were in bed by 11:30 PM 55 percent of the time and up by 9 AM 70 percent of the time.

11. Carnegie Foundation for the Advancement of Teaching, 1990.
12. According to the AnyU Office of Residence Life, of the 3,564 upperclass-men living in the dorms (I exclude family living and freshman dorms) on August 31, 2002, 405 people had moved by December 1, 2003, and by January 31, 2003, 938 people had moved.

3. Community and Diversity

1. Carnegie Foundation for the Advancement of Teaching 1990, 64, 63.
2. Ibid., 48.
3. Carnegie Foundation for the Advancement of Teaching 1990, 49.
4. Ibid., 50
5. Varenne 1977.
6. Putnam 2000.
7. Levine and Cureton 1998, 72.
8. My brief section here hardly does justice to the urgency of race and eth-nicity issues on campus or, for that matter, to the active discrimination experienced by gay and transgendered individuals. For more on the thoughts and experiences of minority and gay students, see Lesage et al. 2002 and Howard and Stevens 2000, and see Tusmith and Reddy 2002 for teachers' challenges with teaching diversity to students.
9. To mitigate such factors as meal plans and off-campus versus on-campus living, which may draw differentially on class and ethnicity, I confined my observations to tables shared in the optional dining areas on campus where either a meal plan card or cash was accepted. I made observations only during the day and from Monday to Friday, when most classes were in session, because these were the times and meals, I figured, that would be least affected by demographic and economic differences among students.
10. Each diner ("who," according to gender and ethnicity) and the number at the table (#) were recorded. Then each person sitting at the table was recorded by gender and specific ethnicity, where possible. The data were then sorted and analyzed by looking at the composition of the table from the diner's point of view and marked as to whether the diner was eating with: (1) no one (the person was sitting alone); (2) females of the same ethnic/power group (SF), males of the same ethnic/power group (SM), or a mixed-gender table of the same ethnic/power group (SX); (2) females (OF) or males (OM) of a different ethnic/power group, a mixed-gender table comprising members of a different ethnic/power group (OX); or (3) a mixed ethnic/power group that was all female (MxF), all male (MxM), or mixed gender (MxX). The term "ethnic/power group" is used because, for purposes of this section, people's ethnicities were analyzed in two broad categories that are more

than ethnic designations: dominant (white non-Hispanic) and minority (people of color) groups. More detailed ethnic information was recorded and reviewed, but the comparisons here focused on dominant and non-dominant groups.

11. "Walk into the cafeteria in most colleges and universities," write Levine and Cureton "and the tables are separated by race and ethnicity. The larger the campus, the sharper the divisions" (1998, 86).

4. As Others See Us

1. Some comments in this chapter appear in edited form. I took notes during international student interviews, and tried to get comments down verbatim, but did not tape the interviews. As a result, I often imposed my own native English on them, so, for instance, a Japanese woman saying, "Excuse but not understand," would be written as "Excuse me but I don't understand." I did not record in my notes "uhs," "you knows," and other interjections and hesitations that would have been preserved in a taped record. This chapter contains many snippets of conversations. For a fuller feeling for the thinking of international students, and more complete narrative from individuals, see Garrod and Davis 1999.

2. I employ the vernacular use of "American" to mean U.S., but, as international students are well aware, there are many countries in the Americas, and making "American" equivalent with only the United States is one aspect of the egocentricity international students identify in the U.S. system. Nevertheless, this term accurately represents how students themselves talk about the United States.

5. Academically Speaking . . .

1. There was only one deviation from the norm in all my classes (out of approximately fourteen total questions posed). When a student asked, "What will we learn in here?" a palpable silence fell over the room.

2. In his discussion of "higher-mindedness," Moffatt (1989), too, mentioned the seeming lack of general discussion about intellectual or academic topics. He assumed, however, that he wasn't hearing these deeper conversations because they weren't shared with professors. I wondered whether it wasn't the same for me as an older, less socially involved student.

3. I purposely did not choose the first or last two weeks of classes or registration weeks, when academic talk about class choices, courses, and professors was probably much more common.

4. Holland and Eisenhart 1990, 211.

5. Holland and Eisenhart, for instance, found that students' peer cultures

were not organized around classes and majors, that friends often didn't even know one another's majors, and that academic progress and related decisions were considered personal business (1990, 14). Moffatt's Rutgers University students separated learning from the classroom, claiming that they "came of age in college thanks to what they learned among themselves on their own" (1989, 54). Even in traditional college culture, described by Horowitz (1987, chap. 2), men valued extracurricular success, in sports and clubs, over classroom achievement.

6. The Art of College Management

1. Horowitz 1987, 34, 36.
2. Ibid., 36.
3. Doing full justice to these cultures, which Horowitz describes as a complex of values, attitudes, and behavior, can be accomplished only by reading Horowitz's work. Here I extract only some central kernels of the cultures as she has described them.
4. Ibid., 269.
5. From an information Web site directed at college students, August 2002.
6. For the uninitiated, Web courses are delivered on-line and are accessed through a student's home computer. The student may "attend" the course at any time, so long as assignments and exams are delivered by specified deadlines. Usually, all information delivery, class discussions, and faculty-student interactions occur on-line so that any schedule can be accommodated.
7. Sixty percent of freshmen reported conversing with professors outside of class, versus 74 percent of seniors. National Survey of Student Engagement 2003.
8. Higher Education Research Institute (2003), a survey developed by HERI and the Policy Center on the First Year of College at Brevard College.
9. National Survey of Student Engagement 2003, 7.
10. Higher Education Research Institute 2003. A total of 30,280 first-time, full-time, first-year students from 136 colleges and universities across the country responded to the instrument.
11. National Survey of Student Engagement 2003, 14.
12. Higher Education Research Institute 2003, fn. 42.
13. McCabe and Trevino 1996.
14. From an information Web site directed at college students, August 2002.
15. McCabe 2004.
16. North Carolina State University 2001.
17. Consistently in national studies, students who said that they never cheated actually reported engaging in one of the behaviors labeled as

cheating. This discrepancy arises because they don't consider all "cheating" behaviors to be cheating. According to North Carolina State University 2001, 52 percent of students nationwide (and 61 percent at N.C. State) report that at least one item of cheating identified on the form is "not cheating." There is, moreover, often wide disagreement between students and faculty about what constitutes cheating (Whitley and Keith-Spiegel 2002).

18. I did not ask what should be taken into consideration in punishing students for cheating, and therefore elicited different answers. Students were asked when it was OK to cheat, and thus emphasized performance issues (such as "when you're failing") and money issues ("If I need extra funds, I write papers for money") but also the ease of cheating ("anytime you can't do the work yourself and know you won't get caught").

19. McCabe 2000, 5.

20. Ibid.

21. North Carolina State University 2001.

22. Another 19 percent see themselves as less interested in the subject as a result of the class.

23. National Survey of Student Engagement 2003.

7. Lessons from My Year as a Freshman

1. There is also the disturbing suggestion here that a faculty member giving voice to student culture and concerns (or a white person giving voice to the black experience) is somehow more credible than a member of that culture.

2. In addition to the one journalism student who kept asking me questions, I revealed my identity to three other students before my research ended. In all four cases I felt that maintaining my secrecy could be damaging to the students involved. I describe these situations in the book's afterword, "Ethics and Ethnography."

3. Higher Education Research Institute 2003.

4. From *http://www.yic.gov/drugfree/alcabuse.html,* accessed July 2004.

5. Moffatt 1989, 90.

6. Whitaker 1996 shows how the characteristic appearance of the American suburb comes out of this dynamic of "choosing to be alike," while Varenne 1977 shows how the distinctions among American Protestant denominations are maintained by the same processes. The articulation of individualism and conformity in American life comes up repeatedly in foreign commentaries on the United States in collections such as De-Vita and Armstrong 2002.

7. After I bought my backpack at a big box store, I remember noticing how

my pack was somehow not "right," at least not the same as other students'. Mine had too many straps and strings and extra pockets; it was nylon and two-colored. Most students that year carried Jansport packs that were smaller and made of a Cordura-type material in a solid color. It was not as if these all came from the same student bookstore, but somehow a tacit knowledge gets communicated about exactly what backpacks should look like.

8. Incidents around the country were well documented on the Web site *http://www.collegefreedom.org/*, accessed August 2004.

9. Moffatt 1989. It is also an allusion to Margaret Mead's *Coming of Age in Samoa*, in which she described Samoan adolescence.

10. Gennep 1960.

11. Turner 1969, 95. Turner calls this "communitas."

12. Turner 1982, 44.

13. U.S. Department of Education 2002, chap. 3, table 183.

14. In 1985–86, state appropriations accounted for 43.2 percent of the total budget of public degree-granting institutions. By 1995–96, state appropriations funded only 32.5 percent of the total budget, a precipitous decline. U.S. Department of Education 2002, table 330, "Current-fund revenue of public degree-granting institutions by source: 1980–1 to 1999–2000."

15. Ibid.

16. According to the "Greater Expectations National Panel Report" of the Association of American Colleges and Universities (2002, viii), 53 percent of students now attending college must take remedial courses.

17. U.S. Department of Education 2002, table 350, "Educational and general expenditures of degree-granting public universities, by purpose: 1976–7 to 1999–2000."

18. For a select group of research universities, the university-corporate relationship in research has been important since World War II. For a fascinating look at how these relationships were cultivated, see Lowen 1997.

19. Now that university presidents are accountable for the bottom lines of their institutions, it is interesting to note that presidential terms at universities have become much like CEO terms in duration, lasting an average of five years. McLaughlin and Riesman 1993, 183.

20. U.S. Department of Education 2002, tables 35 and 312.

21. U.S. Department of Education 2004a.

22. Ibid, 1. During the 1990s, borrowers rose from 30 percent to 45 percent of full-time dependent students.

23. U.S. Department of Education 2002, table 352, "Bachelor's degrees conferred by degree-granting institutions, by discipline division: 1970–71 to 2000–2001."

24. For a detailed account, see McPherson and Schapiro 1999.

25. The reading this particular year was Diane Smith's *Letters from Yellowstone,* but each year the book chosen by the faculty was different—typically contemporary novels converging on freshman seminar themes regarding liberal education. Daniel Quinn's *Ishmael* and James McBride's *Color of Water* have been past selections.
26. From Cronon 1998, reprinted in our freshman seminar reader.

Afterword

1. The one I consulted carefully before undertaking this work was the American Anthropological Association's statement on professional ethics, *www.aaanet.org.*

References

Adler, Patricia, and Peter Adler. 1991. *Backboards and Blackboards*. New York: Columbia University Press.

Altbach, Philip G. 1993. "Students: Interests, Culture, and Activism." In *Higher Learning in America: 1980–2000*, edited by Arthur Levine, 203–21. Baltimore: John Hopkins University Press.

Altbach, Philip G.; Robert O. Berdahl, and Patricia J. Gumport. 1999. *American Higher Education in the Twenty-first Century: Social, Political, and Economic Challenges*. Baltimore: Johns Hopkins University Press.

Association of American Colleges and Universities. 2002. Greater Expectations National Panel Report. *http://www.greaterexpectations.org*.

Astin, Alexander W. 2000. "The American College Student: Three Decades of Change." In *Higher Education in Transition: The Challenges of the New Millennium*, edited by Joseph Losco and Brian I. Fife, 7–28. Westport, Conn.: Bergin & Garvey.

Bell, Inge and Bernard McGrane. 1999. *This Book Is Not Required*. Thousand Oaks, Calif.: Pine Forge Press.

Carnegie Foundation for the Advancement of Teaching. 1990. *Campus Life: In Search of Community*. Princeton: Carnegie Foundation for the Advancement of Teaching.

Clarke-Pearson, Mary. 2001 "Download. Steal. Copy: Cheating at the University." *The Daily Pennsylvanian*. *http://www.dailypennsylvanian.com/vnews/display.v/ART/2001/11/27*.

Cronon, William. 1998. "Only Connect: The Goals of Liberal Education." *American Scholar* 67, no. 4:73–80.

DeVita, Philip R., and James D. Armstrong, eds. 2002. *Distant Mirrors: America as a Foreign Culture*. 3rd edition. Belmont, Calif.: Wadsworth.

Eble, Connie. 1996. *Slang and Sociability: In-Group Language among College Students.* Chapel Hill: University of North Carolina Press.

Garrod, Andrew, and Jay Davis. 1999. *Crossing Customs: International Students Write on U.S. College Life and Culture.* New York: Falmer Press.

Gennep, Arnold van. 1960. *The Rites of Passage.* London: Routledge.

Giroux, Henry A., and Kostas Myrsiades. 2001. *Beyond the Corporate University: Culture and Pedagogy in the New Millennium.* Lanham, Md.: Rowman and Littlefield.

Higher Education Research Institute. 2003. Your First College Year, 2003 Findings, University of California, Los Angeles. *http://www.gseis.ucla.edu/heri/yfcy/yfcy_findings.html.*

Holland, Dorothy C., and Margaret A. Eisenhart. 1990. *Educated in Romance: Women, Achievement, and College Culture.* Chicago: University of Chicago Press.

Horowitz, Helen Lefkowitz. 1987. *Campus Life: Undergraduate Cultures from the End of the Eighteenth Century to the Present.* Chicago: University of Chicago Press.

Howard, Kim, and Annie Stevens. 2000. *Out and About Campus: Personal Accounts by Lesbian, Gay, Bisexual, and Transgendered College Students.* Los Angeles: Alyson Books.

Kjos, Les. 2004. "Cheating Increases on College Campuses." *Washington Times,* January 24, 2004.

Lawton, Millicent. 1998. "At Many Colleges, Dorm Living Is Easy—Though Crowded." *Christian Science Monitor* 90, no. 238 (November 3): B6.

Lesage, Julia, Abby L. Ferber, Debbie Storrs, and Donna Wong. 2002. *Making a Difference: University Students of Color Speak Out.* Lanham, Md.: Rowman & Littlefield.

Levine, Arthur, ed. 1993. *Higher Learning in America: 1980–2000.* Baltimore: Johns Hopkins University Press.

Levine, Arthur, and Jeanette S. Cureton. 1998. *When Hope and Fear Collide: A Portrait of Today's College Student.* San Francisco: Jossey-Bass.

Losco, Joseph, and Brian I. Fife, eds. 2000. *Higher Education in Transition: The Challenges of the New Millennium.* Westport, Conn.: Bergin & Garvey.

Lowen, Rebecca. 1997. *Creating the Cold War University: The Transformation of Stanford.* Berkeley: University of California Press.

McCabe, Donald L. 2000. Interview. "The New Research on Academic Integrity: The Success of 'Modified' Honor Codes." Asheville, N.C.: College Administration Publications. *http://www.collegepubs.com/ref/SFX000515.shtml.*

McCabe, Donald. L., and L. K. Trevino. 1996. "What We Know about Cheating in College: Longitudinal Trends and Recent Developments." *Change* 28, no. 1: 29–33.

McCabe, Donald L., Linda Klebe Trevino, and Kenneth D. Butterfield. 1999.

"Academic Integrity in Honor Code and Non–Honor Code Environments: A Qualitative Investigation." *Journal of Higher Education* 70, no. 2 (March 1): 211–34.

McDonald, William M., and Associates. 2002. *Creating Campus Community: In Search of Ernest Boyer's Legacy.* San Francisco: Jossey Bass.

McLaughlin, Judith Block, and David Riesman. 1993. "The President: A Precarious Perch." In *Higher Learning in America: 1980–2000,* edited by Arthur Levine, 179–202. Baltimore: Johns Hopkins University Press.

McPherson, Michael S., and Morton O. Schapiro. 1999. *Reinforcing Stratification in American Higher Education: Some Disturbing Trends.* Stanford: National Center for Postsecondary Improvement.

Moffatt, Michael. 1989. *Coming of Age in New Jersey: College and American Culture.* New Brunswick: Rutgers University Press.

National Center for Public Policy and Higher Education. 2002a. *Losing Ground: A National Status Report on the Affordability of American Higher Education.* San Jose, Calif.: National Center for Public Policy and Higher Education. *www.highereducation.org/reports/losing_ground/ar1.shtml.*

———. 2002b. *Measuring Up 2002: The State-by-State Report Card for Higher Education.* Washington, D.C, and San Jose, Calif.: The National Center for Public Policy and Higher Education.

National Survey of Student Engagement. 2003. *2003 Overview.* Bloomington, Ind.: Center for Postsecondary Research, Policy, and Planning. *http://www.indiana.edu/~nsse/nsse_2003/overview_2003.htm.*

North Carolina State University. 2001. Academic Integrity at NC State University: Survey Results and Action Plan. Division of Undergraduate Affairs and Office of Student Conduct, October 16, 2001. *http://www.ncsu. edu/undergrad_affairs/assessment/files/projects/acadint/academic_integrity_at_ ncstate.pdf.*

Pattenaude, Richard L. 2000. "Administering the Modern University." In *Higher Education in Transition: The Challenges of the New Millennium,* edited by Joseph Losco and Brian I. Fife, 159–76. Westport, Conn.: Bergin & Garvey.

Pratt, Linda Ray. 2003. "Will Budget Troubles Restructure Higher Education?" *Academe. http://www.aaup.org/publications/Academe/2003/03jf/03jfpra.htm.*

Putnam, Robert D. 2000. *Bowling Alone: The Collapse and Revival of American Community.* New York: Simon & Schuster.

Rojstaczer, Stuart. 2001. "When Intellectual Life Is Optional for Students." *Chronicle of Higher Education* 46, no. 32 (April 20): B5.

Rubington, Earl. 1990. "Drinking in the Dorms: A Study of the Etiquette of RA–Resident Relations." *Journal of Drug Issues* 20, no. 3 (summer): 451–62.

Sanday, Peggy R. 1990. *Fraternity Gang Rape: Sex, Brotherhood, and Privilege on Campus.* New York: New York University Press.

Segal, Carolyn Foster. 2000. "The Dog Ate My Disk, and Other Tales of Woe." *Chronicle of Higher Education* 46 (August 11): A64.

Shumar, Wesley. 1997. *College for Sale: A Critique of the Commodification of Higher Education*. London: Falmer Press.

Siskos, Catherine. 2000. "Home, Sweet Dorm." *Kiplinger's Personal Finance Magazine* 54, no. 8 (August): 26.

Tierney, William G. 1993. *Building Communities of Difference: Higher Education in the Twenty-first Century*. Westport, Conn.: Bergin & Garvey.

Toom, Andrei. 2002. "A Russian Teacher in America." In *Distant Mirrors: America as Foreign Culture*. 3rd ed. Edited by Philip DeVita and James D. Armstrong, chap. 15. Belmont, Calif.: Wadsworth.

Turner, Victor Witter. 1969. *The Ritual Process: Structure and Anti-structure*. Ithaca: Cornell University Press.

———. 1974. *Dramas, Fields, and Metaphors; Symbolic Action in Human Society*. Ithaca: Cornell University Press.

———. 1982. *From Ritual to Theatre: The Human Seriousness of Play*. New York: Performing Arts Journal Publications.

Tusmith, Bonnie, and Maureen T. Reddy, eds. 2002. *Race in the College Classroom: Pedagogy and Politics*. New Brunswick: Rutgers University Press.

U.S. Department of Education. 2002. *Digest of Education Statistics*. Chap. 3. "Postsecondary Education." Washington, D.C.: National Center for Education Statistics. *http://nces.ed.gov/programs/digest/d02/ch_3.asp*.

———. 2004a. *Education Facts from NCES: Highlights from "The Condition of Education, 2004."* Washington, D.C.: National Center for Education Statistics.

———. 2004b. *Paying for College: Changes between 1990 and 2000 for Full-Time Dependent Students*. Findings from the Status of Education Report 2004. Washington, D.C.: U.S. Department of Education.

Varenne, Hervé. 1977. *Americans Together: Structured Diversity in a Midwestern Town*. New York: Teachers College Press.

Whitaker, Craig. 1996. *Architecture and the American Dream*. New York: Three Rivers Press.

White, Geoffry D., with Flannery Hauck, eds. 2000. *Campus Inc.: Corporate Power in the Ivory Tower*. Amherst, N.Y.: Prometheus.

Whitley, Bernard E, and Patricia Keith-Spiegel. 2002. *Academic Dishonesty: An Educator's Guide*. Mahwah, N.J.: Erlbaum Associates.

Wilgoren, Jodi. 2000. Close Quarters. *New York Times Magazine*, August 27: 24.

Index

About the Author

Rebekah Nathan is a Ph.D. in anthropology who has conducted extensive overseas fieldwork. She currently is a professor of anthropology and graduate coordinator at "AnyU," where she teaches both graduate and undergraduate courses.